Marcel Beyer, born in Tailfingen/Württemberg in 1965, grew up in Kiel and Neuss. He studied German and English literature in Siegen, writing an MA thesis on the poet Friederike Mayröcker in 1992. A poet, essayist and novelist, he has also translated poetry by Gertrude Stein and Michael Hofmann. Marcel Beyer has received numerous awards including Germany's most prestigious, the Georg Büchner Prize. He has lived in Dresden since 1996.

Katy Derbyshire translates contemporary German writers including Olga Grjasnowa, Selim Özdoğan and Heike Geissler. Her translation of Clemens Meyer's Bricks and Mortar was nominated for the MAN Booker International Prize and won her the Straelen Translation Prize. She teaches literary translation and also heads the V&Q Books imprint. She has lived in Berlin since 1996.

Putin's Postbox

Marcel Beyer

Translated from German by Katy Derbyshire

V&Q BOOKS

BERLIN 🐻

Senate Department
for Culture and Europe

Funded by Berlin Senate Department for Culture
and Europe

V&Q Books, Berlin 2022
An imprint of Verlag Voland & Quist GmbH
First published in the German language as
Marcel Beyer, *Putins Briefkasten – Acht Recherchen*

Translation © Katy Derbyshire
Editing: Florian Duijsens
Copy editing: Angela Hirons
Cover photo © Unsplash
Cover design: Pingundpong*Gestaltungsbüro
Typesetting: Fred Uhde
Printing and binding: PBtisk, Příbram, Czech Republic

ISBN: 978-3-86391-332-8

www.vq-books.eu

I

On an impulse not quite clear to myself, this morning I got in the car almost still drowsy and drove out to the edge of town to take another look at a certain originally maize-yellow but now moss-green postbox, the image of which has been in my mind since last winter. That box, I remember precisely, is installed next to the entrance to an otherwise unremarkable block of flats, and it is one of the rather unattractive models that were fitted everywhere in West Germany, mainly in the 1980s, when right angles were considered uncontemporary and rounded corners were preferred, which, however, didn't make the postboxes look more elegant but, on the contrary, clunkier.

When I first went looking for the block with the postbox, I had trouble finding the address – number 101 on Radeberger Strasse, a street that thins down to an unpaved road, then dwindles to a trodden path. The entire prefabricated housing estate is in an area that may once not have been marked on the map of Dresden at all, or merely as a blank spot, for to a certain extent it was a part of Russia – and by my impression, it still is today – albeit a piece of Russia that is unlikely to be marked on any Russian map. During the latter half of the 80s, a flat on the third floor of the building at 101 Radeberger Strasse, once called Julian-Marchlewski-Strasse, with the postbox I recalled affixed to its façade by the Deutsche Bundespost after 1990, possibly in 1992, immediately after the last Commonwealth of Independent States troops left Dresden, was home to the Putin family.

The house numbers and entrances – as I've known since that winter, when I saw numerous footprints in the snow – are on the rear side of the long building, located on a street with no name. Upon turning onto that bumpy lane, I find confirmation of an inkling that came to me on the way; the postbox has indeed been removed since I was last here. Not even plastered-over drill holes are visible in the concrete slab dividing the ground-floor living room from the outside world, I establish, as I ascend the three steps between the clearly demarcated patches of lawn on either side of the front door.

All apartments but one appear to be occupied, as I gather from the doorbell panel – 12 parties in total. For the second-floor flat on the right – perhaps the one underneath that of Vladimir Putin – the label states: 'guest apartment'; perhaps because it's hard to rent out, because tenants can't stand the thought of the ghost of a long-vanished Russian trampling about above their heads; perhaps because guests – *whose* guests? I wonder – might enjoy spending a night or two imagining a sleepless president-to-be pacing the floor upstairs.

That seems exaggerated, however; it simply doesn't befit a man always described as extremely inconspicuous, if not to say faceless. This invisibility can't be solely due to his work as a secret service officer either; it must be down to his person, for he is a man whose life provides so little anecdotal material that his biographers regard it as noteworthy that members of a Dresden anglers' club recalled only one characteristic of their new recruit from Leningrad: his unbearable pedantry. He stuck stoically to his views, they reported, for instance on how to affix bait correctly to the hook, or how the line had to be cast out at a particular angle, for which reason his clubmates were on the brink of losing all joy in the not exactly joyful art of angling.

While I take a look around and make notes, I am observed from one of the upper windows, by an old woman, I suspect – I don't look up very closely. She was presumably already watching me as I parked my car in the residents' parking area, got out and cast a glance through the glass door into the stairwell; as I strode along the block, nine entrances in total, recognisable from a distance by the reddish matte facing which extends six storeys up the otherwise evenly grey façade; as I turned left, having reached the far end of the block, as I spied a decrepit building, perhaps a former school, appearing between the already sparsely leafed trees. And she watches me still, as I walk back down the gentle slope to my car, where birches, maples and beeches grow wild behind the windscreen.

Here, secluded from the city, Russian is still spoken as a matter of course, as I hear when a young couple heads towards me. Only a schoolboy behind me has fun reciting the numbers one to ten in loud English, and as he passes, he says, 'Bad boys, bad boys,' shaping his hand into a gun, setting his sights on me and then issuing a few muted assault rifle sounds.

The postbox is no longer there, I note down before starting up the engine, and I think: the old woman on the fifth floor will soon have her peace and quiet again. As I drive slowly past bottle banks and an abandoned three-piece suite, towards Elbtal, and put that empty Russian space behind me, the anecdotal far from my mind, it occurs to me that I may well have provided the woman at the window with enough material for her to spend the rest of the day fabricating an anecdote to tell her husband when he returns home in the evening, as they're sitting at the table and eating an unremarkable meal like something that might have been served in the neighbouring flat at the end of the 1980s, in the Putin family.

*

The Grosser Garten is on the south-eastern edge of Dresden's old centre. It is the town's largest inner-city park, a place you can take your Sunday walks for years at a time without ever getting the impression you've seen every group of plants, every copse and every cutting – although the Great Garden occupies a straightforward rectangle on the map and is largely structured along clear lines in its mixture of baroque garden and English park. The Grosser Garten is perhaps the counterpoint to the Ostragehege, or, as Caspar David Friedrich called his famous painting: *The Great Enclosure at Dresden*, an area on the other side of the old city, to the west and, as we can see in Friedrich's work – his sunset sky mirrored in a web of pools and puddles – an alluvial plain of the Elbe, a peri-urban wilderness devoid of right angles into which the Dresdeners rarely venture, or so it appears when viewing the Ostra Enclosure from the opposite bank on a walk along the Elbe.

The name Ostragehege has an echo of *Ost*, the east, and it is in fact of Slavic origin, just as Dresden's name goes back to a Slavic word for swamp dwellers – this city with its old wards like Seidnitz, Loschwitz, Leubnitz and Kleinzschachwitz is nothing more than an agglomeration of Slavic settlements built on swampland.

The Grosser Garten, in contrast, was created not on a drained swamp but on fields outside the city, originally as a site for baroque feasts, staged hunts for red deer or bears driven through wooded scenery, with no place to hide in the thickets or to escape to altogether. To this day, the Grosser Garten performs the wilderness in consistently domesticated form, as tamed as nature appears in the adjacent Zoological Garden – or at least separated from curious visitors by bars, ditches and panes of glass. Which does not mean the wilderness disappears with the dividing line between man and beast – sometimes a glance suffices to encourage a barely recognisably wild creature, living out its years as jaded children's entertainment, to mime its wildness again.

For instance in 1867, when the Dostoevskys – on this rare occasion not short on funds – are subjected to a staging of wildness on a visit to the Dresden zoo that far exceeds what you might expect for the entrance fee. As his wife noted in her diary, Dostoevsky seeks eye contact with a one-eyed male beast in the lion house, stares it in the eye and is in turn stared back at by the lion, stands up to the lion's glare without batting an eyelid, and forces the mighty creature, through this play of the eyes, to express its wildness: the lion begins to roar wildly, yet Dostoevsky's leonine glare stands up, the lion roars and roars until the lionesses add their growls to the choir. Whereupon all present are mightily impressed, the lion family just as much as the wife and Dostoevsky himself: the expressive Russian writer has stared into the African lion's soul, forcing it without a word, not a single Russian word, to externalise its interior, to break out in leonine expression.

But what are we really dealing with in this story, told by Hans Blumenberg in his *Lions* book? Is it praise for a husband perhaps unmighty in everyday life, but certainly mighty on a visit to the zoo? Praise for the wordless understanding between man and beast, of which only an extremely sensitive mind is capable? Or praise for the Russian language, which proves mighty even when it isn't spoken at all?

No, I believe the visit to the Dresden zoo described in Anna Dostoevsky's diary bears the traces of an experience that can be read through another writer's observation, noted almost a hundred years later. It is Elias Canetti who – without thinking of the Dostoevskys' flight across Europe, through foreign language territories – once described, in conjunction with considerations on keeping a diary, what influence travel may exert on our ideas of language. According to Canetti, our perspective on both our own and unfamiliar languages alters abruptly in foreign lands, when speaking to strangers without understanding one another; that is, when attempting to make ourselves understood by means of signs and pretended words. And he writes in 1965, as if commenting on that 1867 lion scene: 'Language, otherwise an instrument that one thought one could manipulate, suddenly becomes wild and dangerous.'

In unfamiliar lands, our own language proves to be the untameable lion itself.

*

From west to east, the Grosser Garten is divided by the broad main boulevard into two equal-sized areas, its northern and southern halves. A while ago, I began to notice on my walks that this boulevard marks not only the middle of the park, but also a linguistic border – my Sunday language border when I walk around the northern part, coming from the south. Entering the park from Tiergartenstrasse at the Carola Pond on Sunday afternoons, I find myself in the midst of excursionists: families, groups, couples visiting the Carola Palace, the restaurant on the lake, disembarking from the nearest park railway station or renting a rowing boat. A tangle of voices from which I pick up German words and phrases at every turn.

From the Carola Pond, I follow the canal to the north. The park grows quieter, cyclists and skaters crossing the main path. Beyond the main path, towards the New Pond, the sound of the language surrounding me shifts all at once: Russian mingles with German, and the proportion of Russian increases the closer I get to the northern edge of the Grosser Garten.

For a time, it seemed as though the linguistic boundary in the Grosser Garten were impermeable to the south, as though Dresden's Russophone inhabitants, who live in Johannstadt in the north, only ever walked as far as the main path, or else they fell silent as soon as they followed the paths into the southern part of the park.

Gradually, though, very gradually with each passing Sunday, the boundary has been shifting. Whereas the first Russian words I heard on the southern side were a sensation, I now keep an eye out for groups of people, and wager with myself whether they will speak German or Russian amongst themselves. The language is migrating. And the languages are mingling. Although today's Russian is, of course, a 'different' Russian to that spoken in Dresden until the early 1990s, or which, more frequently still, remained unheard: the Russian of the Soviet troops garrisoned here, who rarely left their barracks and then usually in closed groups, whose best-known former member these days is Vladimir Putin.

*

How does that untameable lion, our own language in foreign climes, react when it feels threatened, for instance by an unruly mob shouting and jeering in anger? Does it go on the attack, or does another creature leap – so swiftly that hardly anyone notices – into its place?

On 5 December 1989, Vladimir Putin and his colleagues are intently incinerating files at their office. Every regime so far has learned from experience that paper does not burn well in large quantities, since the flames barely get enough oxygen to nourish them, but every regime apparently has to experience this anew. Perhaps the KGB staff in Dresden soaked their heaps of files in the famous Russian tank fuel; in any case, dense smoke forms on the grounds, rising above Bautzner Strasse and drawing a curious crowd that day, of demonstrators in the process of storming the Stasi headquarters around the corner. Later, Vladimir Putin will describe it in leonine terms, saying it was perfectly alright for him to watch the Germans tear their own secret service to pieces.

Putin explains to the unruly mob that this is not a German but a Soviet institution – they have got the wrong address, so to speak. They don't trust him. Someone asks: 'And who are you? You speak such good German.'

One might think the lamb had taken the place of the lion without the demonstrators noticing: speak the foreign language on foreign territory to convince you are tame. Especially as Vladimir Putin speaks a domesticated German, the German of language courses, and not the Saxon German of the streets of Dresden – that, too, may be the source of surprise at his 'good German'.

What he hasn't reckoned with is the fact that the German language arouses the demonstrators' distrust on this occasion, this particular evening. It exposes him to the suspicion of being a Stasi agent, despite his High German camouflage. Were he to speak in Russian – who knows, perhaps the unruly Dresdeners would be prepared, after a few easily comprehensible sentences, to regard him as a local Gorbachev. No one out there in front of the KGB office knows, after all, that Putin is merely improvising, that he envisaged everything very differently. In fact, armed security forces were to be in his place. But when he went to call them, the curt response was: 'We can't do anything without orders from Moscow. And Moscow is silent.' Not a single word of Russian on the telephone line. Even Moscow no longer speaks Putin's language.

'And who are you?' There is no record of whether the secret service agent gives his name in this situation, as he speaks with a tamed German tongue rather than falling back into familiar Russian. He is a translator, he says. Simply a translator.

*

It is said Vladimir Putin still enjoys practising the foreign language he learned back then, when he visits Germany – and perhaps in his mind's eye, while he chats with the chancellor, he sees those heaps of files smouldering.

I've never heard him speak, nor do I know how freely he actually moved around Dresden, whether a secret service officer was permitted, for instance, to leave the garrison with his wife on a Sunday afternoon purely for pleasure – but a KGB man is always on the job. Yet in retrospect, Putin's character seems to stand out from the mass of Dresden's Russians in so many facets that I wouldn't put it past him: excursions to the Grosser Garten, which over time come to seem, perhaps not to his wife but to his colleagues, like minor dares, small adventures, secretly permitted by his superiors, of course, as a reward for outstanding work, or simply in recognition of his general inconspicuousness, nothing of which will change, even on a Sunday in the city.

The Putins overstepping the boundary: In the northern half of the park, the couple speak Russian, but as soon as they reach the main path he swaps to German, as if pressing a switch, not interrupting his wife's chatter. He, a master of camouflage and adaptation as a secret service agent, and she, the wife of that master, thus stride in a southerly direction for a while, Lyudmila Putina never letting on that she may barely understand a word of her husband's. Nodding gently, I imagine, she walks by his side – her silent pride and silent observation of the fellow strollers they pass: do they notice that this not very tall man with the sober expression is not a native German speaker?

15

And then I see the two of them – her arm now locked beneath his, tugging him gently onto a side path to the right – vanishing between the trees towards the zoo, where they will visit their secret Dostoevsky memorial in the lion house as they do every Sunday.

This man doesn't smoke, doesn't drink; the military police won't have to pull this man inebriated out of a bush in the Grosser Garten in the early hours of Monday morning. This man stands silent in front of the lion's cage – and who knows, perhaps when no one but them is in the lion house, he swiftly opens his mouth wide for his wife's sake, in commemoration of a great Russian writer and in expectation of his own role in the decades to come.

*

Never have I seen Vladimir Putin in an overcoat. He makes appearances in an impeccably fitting agent's suit, or alternatively in a practical all-weather jacket of the kind that has now conquered the world after starting out in provincial German towns, or in a flying jacket with a fur collar straight out of a vodka ad; he shows himself in a diving suit, in a snug existentialist's jersey or preferably with a bare chest.

As though a comment of Dostoevsky were haunting him: 'We all come from Gogol's "Overcoat"' – stretching from the 19th century into the 20th, from Lenin's overcoat to Ceaușescu's, those dark, heavy winter coats that augur nothing but night, and cold, and downfall and, in the end, a few splashes of blood on the sturdy fabric. The leather Gestapo overcoat, almost touching the ground. Joseph Beuys' shaman coat.

We all come from Gogol's *Overcoat*? Vladimir Putin, though, is determined not to cloak himself in that overcoat; he has discarded it, and it seems to me he means it to signal that – despite the nostalgia for the USSR which he summons up in the service of Soviet veterans – he has understood: that century proceeding from the 19th into the 20th is now behind us for good.

II

On one occasion, we drive hundreds of kilometres east in the November fug to visit the border town of Narva. We want to see the river of the same name, which divides Estonia from Russia, and a place we were told in Tallinn was probably the bleakest anywhere in the world. Essentially, Narva is a Russian city on the Estonian side; almost all its inhabitants speak Russian, and most are dependent on a single employer, a textiles factory that rules over the town. Clothing for the whole world is manufactured in Narva.

In my memory, the city is greyish-brown and black. At this time of year, there are six hours of light a day, and were the sea not nearby, one might think no sky existed at all above Narva.

I don't see any pigeons and yet I can't help thinking of these birds, the unpopular cohabitants of our cities, despised by many. The people in Narva seem to me like unloved cohabitants of their own town. The elderly women on the bank of the Narva, from where they have a view of the border bridge, the dark town on the opposite side, then nothing more: barren land all the way to Saint Petersburg. What are they waiting for with their shopping bags as the sun sets; what are they looking for over there between the tower blocks in nearby Russia?

A little later, the city fills up with people; the workers returning home from the textile plant at the end of the day shift. Someone told us they get their food through a hatch at work, food as bad as the pay. The textile plant has, of course, not been a Soviet factory for many years now. It belongs to a consortium from Asia and, should the workforce demand better conditions, the owners threaten to relocate to Russia – to the other bank of the Narva, where wages are even lower than here.

Fuel shortages, soot, cheap drugs, and every day the same slop. In the middle of Narva's grey post-shift bustle, a child's anorak catches my eye: pale-blue fabric decorated with white polar bears following each other around the jacket with their heads raised in a friendly manner. Always in a circle, walking curiously after each other, and never does one polar bear barge into another.

The child vanishes in the crowd, boards a bus, a front door closes behind him – I can't quite remember, but the anorak seems familiar, an echo I can't place at first as we leave the city in darkness, hundreds of kilometres ahead of us, by night.

One August night in 1992, I am sitting at Warschauer Strasse station in Berlin. It is four in the morning; the first train of the day will take me back west to Wannsee in half an hour. To keep me awake, I smoke one cigarette after another. It grows cool. I note down a sentence; what prompted it escapes my memory: 'You have to be able to see at night too, otherwise nothing will become of you.' I wrap myself in my summer jacket and stare dully across the tracks.

The platform lights go off, my train arrives, and it's only on my way back to West Berlin that I realise I had in my sight all along, an advertising slogan towering above a wall outside the station. In large letters, it says: NARVA TAGHELL – as bright as day.

NARVA, an acronym – with N standing for nitrogen, AR for argon, VA for vacuum: light bulbs that must have illuminated me as I sat there, turned towards sleep and, I thought, away from language.

Today, I wonder whether that early morning at a station on the border between East and West Berlin was the secret reason for taking that trip to Narva many years later. Perhaps I had to drive for hours through sad, monotonous Estonian countryside because I wanted to rediscover a word on the border with Russia.

As far as I know, all children, no matter what linguistic surroundings they grow up in, play a game at a certain phase of their development that is referred to in German – by Freud, among others – as *fort/da*: gone/here. The irrepressible joy, incomprehensible for some adults, shown by a small child who can't yet speak, when he throws a beloved object, makes it disappear from his view, only to fetch it back from the depths of the world. *Fort/da*: I exert power over things and people, I intervene in the world of things, make objects vanish from the face of the earth and magic them back, I plumb the depths of space.

Later, once the child begins to speak, he no longer needs to throw objects; he learns the power of language, with the aid of which he can call real people and call up unreal objects in his imagination.

Fort/da: an image for the shift between absence and presence, hard to put more concisely in German. But here too, a foreign word is concealed: the Russian *da* – the great, world-spanning *yes*.

Let us assume the imaginary child grows up in Narva. Every day, he says *da* as naturally as *nyet*. And let us imagine he will, when he starts school, wear a pale-blue anorak on which polar bears form a never-ending caravan.

The reason why the pattern seemed so familiar occurred to me later, at home in our flat in Dresden, when I found a folder containing a number of textile designs. Large pieces of hand-painted cardboard on which elephants, tigers, and the aforementioned polar bears cross red, yellow, and pale-blue worlds respectively. How it happened that an Asian company at some point had children's anoraks made in these designs on the Estonian-Russian border, I'm sure no one could say. The cardboard sheets are slightly battered at the edges – they have a long road behind them, having moved house frequently in their near-forgotten folder. According to the fashion calendar, they date back to time immemorial, and had my wife not designed them, I would know as little of their origin as a Russian-speaking textile worker in Estonia.

*

Can we translate into another language the name of the city of Narva, which has passed through Danish, Russian, Estonian and German hands and tongues over nearly a thousand years, when at the same time it contains the name of a light-bulb factory?

Can the station 'Warschauer Strasse' be translated into Polish – it does mean Warsaw Street, after all – and if so, is it still in Berlin? We can at least translate 'Ljubljana' into 'Laibach' without it leaving its location. Things get difficult in the other direction, though: How would I translate, for example – into any language – 'I drive my old Moskva through Catalonia while listening to Laibach?'

The landscapes I cruise through in my car are landscapes of rubble – overgrown, exposed and once again overgrown rubble like that of the *Tower of Babel*, as Juan Benet described it so impressively. A writer from Spain stands in the Kunsthistorisches Museum in Vienna in front of a picture by the Dutch painter Brueghel. He is magically drawn to a painting with a subject characteristic of the art of northern Europe – in the Prado, Benet notes, the tower isn't shown in a single picture from the Spanish schools. 'The collapse of the Babylonian construction was the end of Latin as an imposed and incomprehensible language,' he writes in his reflection on the tower – no language now rules over another; languages can move freely, migrate, exchange words, rub up against each other.

Since the collapse of the Tower of Babel, every text needs its translator, no matter in what language it was written, and regardless of whether it is ever actually translated into another language. Every single piece of literature testifies to this inherent dimension: the echo of other languages. It is even possible to translate texts back into their original language without ever having read them in a foreign language; I am convinced of it.

*

Words – isolated from their language environment, snapped up, not understood – can be fiery nuclei. Nuclei not only of linguistic history, but of 20th-century European history. They maintain their temperature, not cooling down over time; we commit them to memory because they cannot be extinguished with semantics. Take, for instance, the word I found in Marguerite Duras, a place name and yet not the name of any place: *Noyeswarda*.

The word points diffusely eastwards, first of all, and secondly to a historical present, to a moment of life-or-death importance. Marguerite Duras notes it in her book *La Douleur*, which records in journal form the time from April 1945 on, as Duras is waiting in Paris for her husband's return from the liberated Buchenwald concentration camp. She reports over and over to the city reception camp, where the lorries arrive from Germany, studying over and over the faces of the former inmates and prisoners-of-war on the truck beds, hoping and fearing like the countless other women by the side of the road. As soon as a lorry appears, place names are called out, camp names: 'Stalag VII A?' the women ask, 'Kommando Stalag III A?' They call: 'Kassel?' and the strange German place name 'Noyeswarda'. In a footnote, Duras comments: 'I haven't been able to find this name in the atlas. I've probably spelled it as it sounded to me.'

'Noyeswarda' does not in fact appear on any German map. Yet the name reminded me, living in Dresden and having developed an ear for strange-sounding place names that on closer inspection harbour a foreign-language moment, of the town of Hoyerswerda. As if the word's initial sound, the H clearly audible to Germans, had been typically erased in the French calls of those Parisian women, and replaced with an N.

The East as a world initially existing only in words – a relative East dependent on your location, of course: the words become foreign, you become uncertain whether you hear 'correctly' as you enter a sphere of unfamiliar articulations. 'Noyeswarda', expression of hope and fear all at once: from there, from the East, is where the lorries will come.

*

Today, when I travel beyond the boundaries of the world I grew up in, I'm often gripped by a dizzying whirl rather resembling that feeling familiar from childhood, the sensation created on a swing. Something in the abdominal region, hard to describe and, for the child, something that needs no words. Back then, you might say, I discovered time. I'm never quite sure: am I excited, do I feel sick? Swinging into the sky, one thing's for certain: the earth is behind me, that's where I'll return. My own strength interacting with the force of gravity, I sense: I have the power to swing myself into an oscillation of time; now I'm up, now I'm down, and now I'm up again. A never-ending sequence of 'nows', perhaps only bearable because the dimension of space remains unaffected. I won't leave the perimeter of this swing. Were the chain to break and I to fly through the air untethered, the sequence of nows would also break. The collision with the ground one last now: the end.

For me to get into that whirl today, the unity of place needn't be maintained; quite the opposite, I feel it precisely when I leave my usual location and head towards one compass point: East. This adult dizziness – I still couldn't say whether it feels blissful or unpleasant – has a great deal to do with typography.

A typeface is always a promise. The shop signs, the advertising logos, the hoardings, as soon as I pass the border and drive along country roads into the heartland: what catches my eye is the grotesque lettering of times past. 'Futura' is one of those sans-serif typefaces, and wherever used, it also always signifies what is inherent to its name: these letters point the way to the future. I admire the unfamiliar neon letters in cities, the writing on a wall, the name of a shop stretched above a display window. No, I don't speak Polish, and when I read *teraz*, I automatically think of the German *Terrasse* or terrace, patio. Where I barely understand more than the Polish for warning, drinks and cigarettes, where I can decipher only single words such as *tramwaj* for tram, and *ksero* for xerox, my eye catches on the letters. Not their content, but their form. I've rarely felt that to be a disadvantage; meaning can be distracting.

I see welded seams, frosted glass, pigments, corrosion. The company name on the gate of an abandoned factory, paint dulled over years. Or a single sans-serif H, a black letter on a white background, flanked by strips of red. A sheet-metal sign in the middle of a field, behind it patches of snow, bare shrubs, cranes jutting into a blanket of clouds on the horizon, the subtle shades of grey, the shipyard in Gdańsk. Sure, the inscriptions fade over time, walls are painted over, names familiar from the West begin to shine out from the façades. Yet some remnants persevere.

There, for instance, the sequence of metal letters at a forgotten country crossroads. Perhaps a brand name, perhaps an everyday object; I'd have to guess. It might mean 'grass', no, more likely 'wheat' or, to match the circumstances, 'weeds', dandelions flowering amidst the wild grasses around its base. The word could mean 'freedom'. But I don't guess; the mere shape of the letters captivates me, their almost elegant blockishness, and from a kneeling position one might think the writing had been stamped out of the cloudless sky. Heavy, unalterable: for eternity. To date, time has confirmed the letters; since the early 1990s, though so much has changed fundamentally, no one has thought to dismantle them.

Fonts like these were once used to herald the future, a future that seemed within reach: modernity. And here I feel the dizzy whirl. I know, we all know, that particular future has long since passed.

In July 1914, Joseph Conrad heads east. He had hesitated to accept the invitation to Kraków, and he hesitates still in his account of the journey. I've read 15 pages, and the Conrad family has only made it to London as yet – so many memories tied to the city, English weather and the weather on the North Sea, the family boards the ship, the father stares at the waves and sees himself as a young seaman again, and yet the account is titled 'Poland Revisited'. Conrad postpones the continent, postpones his old Polish name, and it takes him another nine pages before he finally writes: 'We arrived in Cracow late at night.'

It will have long been dark. Fortunately, his present day accompanied him to Kraków, his family, enveloping him like a cocoon as he is pushed into the past. They are exhausted. Something to eat at the hotel. Then the family will retire. But Joseph Conrad knows there can be no thought of sleep. Thankfully, children never want to go to bed early, especially if they can accompany their father on a night-time stroll. In this city, Conrad writes, he ceased to be a child, and laid down a store of memories that he left behind when he went to sea and broke violently with the past. He can be grateful that no one will ask who needs the companion more: the son walking the dark streets of a foreign city, or the father looking his own youth in the eye.

Midnight. Aside from a white-gloved policeman, there's not a soul on the streets. The gloves make his large hands glow in the dark; the officer turns to look at the two foreigners speaking English. There are eight pages to go. The memories come, secret street names, the route to school, an 11-year-old boy in the winter of 1868, in the evenings the two nuns nursing his father, barely a sound in the sick room, which is to become the death room. Back then, Joseph Conrad explains to his son, it was reading that saved him. The future, that was nothing but horror. Then the boy walks the streets of Kraków again, seeing himself cocooned in nothingness, before him the hearse and behind him the funeral procession, a mild afternoon in May. Now Joseph Conrad wants to rush back to the hotel.

He must allow himself time, must immerse himself slowly in the old world. He arranges to meet former schoolmates, talks to like-minded people, discovers to his astonishment that the memory of his father is still alive. Little by little, he edges into the past, ventures out of the cocoon of the family and the present. Conrad at the university library; to his surprise, letters from his father to a close friend have appeared, in which he writes a great deal about his son. Conrad casts a first glance at them: his parents' happy days together, the four-year-old child. Over the course of the coming weeks, copies are to be made of all the letters.

And then: the first of August 1914. The present. The summer stay in the countryside outside Kraków is cancelled. Out of the city, out of the country, back to England. The shock sits deep, and it will take the Conrad family several months to get home, the rushed departure followed by a time of inaction in the Polish mountains, then Vienna, then Genoa, onto a ship and finally to safety. No more pondering his own youth, his father's letters: 'the past had [...] been eclipsed by the tremendous actuality.' A state of shock, yes, and fear – but to me, something else seems to resonate breathlessly on these last pages. A touch of relief. The plan to immerse himself in the past, to summon childhood memories, that plan which Conrad postponed for so long, is swept away all at once – due to, or perhaps a little thanks to, the external circumstances of world politics.

On the night before the first of August, Joseph Conrad is part of a group of men sitting together in the hotel's smoking room. The shutters are closed, voices from the street; apparently the whole city is on its feet until far into the night. No one has switched on the electric lights, only a few candles illuminating the large room, just bright enough to recognise the next man's face. A typical Conrad setup: any moment now, into the silence, one of those present will dive into his past and begin to tell his story. That night, however: nothing. 'All the past was gone, and there was no future, whatever happened.'

As if someone had chased these elderly gentlemen, sitting motionless in their armchairs – limbs and tongues lamed – into a children's playground, forced them to take a seat on the swing and angle their far-too-long legs. They were given a firm push and now they are swinging involuntarily back and forth, so hard and fast that they feel sick: now, now, and now.

I've never feared modernity. By that I mean less the social utopia connected with it, less the at times rather shrill tone of great promise. The pathos of new departure alienates me, no matter from which side, and even Gothic-type ideas have been set in sans-serif on occasion. No, for me, the leftover fonts of the avant-garde in public space do not herald new departures; they establish, with all due dispassion, that change is underway. They were ill-suited to the time when the inscriptions were made, and I still sense today, whenever I see these letters' clear contours, how the tenses interlock. That's when the dizziness sets in, that's when melancholia comes, if I'm not dragged into the abyss. Neither past nor present nor future will ever be cosy.

I come from a country that has rediscovered Gothic type in recent years. Probably only in part in the sense of a political statement – I see it instead as an indeterminate reaction to an indeterminate fear of the future. In earlier times, I came across such antiquated, antiquating fonts almost exclusively in restaurant names, 'HUBERTUSSTUBEN' set above a pub door in stiff, angular, copper-coloured letters: a siren script for excursionists from industrial regions, they pointed the way to cosiness, into a protective space against the modern world. People my age would rarely have stumbled into the regulars' effluvia, the smell of beer foam and cold cigarette air.

These days, even car showrooms and software sellers advertise their wares in such fonts – not genuine Gothic type, of course, but letters cut on a computer, more a recollection of something no one can read any longer. Even a classic Antiqua appears to awaken fears of the future. No consumer would put up with anything less than the latest technology when choosing a car or an operating system, yet they feel drawn to a vague 'back then' that seems to lie before the invention of the automobile, before the beginning of electronic data processing.

Grotesque types that were installed in public space on the Polish side after 1945, visible to all – those will have partly been a gesture to the West: don't expect any more Gothic letters this side of the border. And where I discover contemporary Gothic lettering beside a Polish country road, laser-printed onto a sign, I take it as a joke and a warning: watch out, this restaurant attracts sentimental tourists. What attracts *me* – 'WITAMINKA' – is a sprightly curved name above a cocktail bar, exhaling fresh air in my direction. There, I know, luminous jelly in futuristic colours awaits me in a glass cabinet.

There are some who pore over the parts of the world map they can only travel with their index fingers, while others stick to the section of the atlas where they live. Until the end of the Cold War, I was part of that latter group; I didn't look East until 1990. The Oder and Neisse were not rivers for me; they were mere words murmured sadly by stubborn old men. I could have summed up my idea of the world beyond my atlas as follows: folk-dancing troupes forcing well-trained smiles every evening, spreading forced jollity to Western tourists while a metallic tour-guide voice reels off historical dates, names and locations no outsider could place or grasp the unspoken meaning of. All you know is that they are tiring, very tiring, as you experience the moment the first date is mentioned. Hence, perhaps, the rehearsed vitality and artificial quaintness, the garish costumes of the evening's folklore performance; to provide a necessary balance to the grey names and numbers of the day's tiring tour. Once you finally get to bed, you're quite exhausted by all the folk music and metallic speeches. But you still won't be able to sleep.

Nothing in this image I had of Eastern Europe drew me in. Folkloric dance troupes have never interested me, and if I feel the need, I can hear reeled-off dates all over the world.

I find it hard to explain, even to myself, the reason my curiosity about Eastern Europe was suddenly piqued in late 1989, early 1990. Certainly, the trigger was the breath-taking changes in that very short time: From a distance, I suddenly saw images I hadn't known before, beamed out of that part of the world previously present on my map as no more than an evenly coloured space. It might have remained a sensation that dies down as quickly as the impressions fade. Yet I was awake – not sleepless and harassed as though I'd spent my evenings watching compulsory folk-dancing – but gripped by the desire for a different perspective. Not exoticism. Not well-meaning openness to the unknown. And neither was it the hope of encountering some familiar thing there I had long thought lost.

Perhaps my new focus on all points East simply emerged from my stance on writing – the only explanation that seems plausible in the end. I work from the margins, partly very literally as I build my sentences; for instance when I start with the name of a colour rather than a noun, to explore how the sentence might be steered from there to a subject. In my reading, I am drawn to the outliers or, as malicious claims would have it, to the obscure. Central books: that is, those everyone can agree on, have never much interested me. I am rarely tempted to explore the centre of my world in writing, and even if I did want to encroach upon a centre, I would have to choose a path from the outside. But outside, too, we advance to the heart of things.

Just as I've always sought territories beyond my own familiar boundaries in my writing, I now leave my old atlas behind me as

33

I travel. And I land unexpectedly at the centre of our continent. Travel, listening, and watching affect my writing in turn. Without these explorations, I would barely pursue the questions I am addressing here; questions of time shifts, time lags, and the use of times and tenses. The consequences are visible too in my dealings with grammar, when I must occasionally think long and hard whether to decide on the present, the perfect or the imperfect.

Travelling beyond the map of my youth, and then, once there, beyond the hotel's tourist map. I'm searching, but not for an abyss; the wet remains of a snowdrift may suffice, in the midst of a fallow piece of land. Hence, I stand today before a metal sign, held up by iron rods rammed into the frosty ground; on the sign, in a clear black font, the single letter H, its meaning unknown to me.

The cranes are not visible from here, but I can make out the gates to the shipyard behind the net curtains. The newly opened pub directly on Solidarność Square has a dozen tables, 15 at most, a realistic expectation in terms of throngs of shipyard workers, and although their work shifts are clearly changing over, we've seen only a few passing through the gates. I feel a mighty sense of melancholy. What music would suit? Neither folkloric party favourites nor the greatest hits of all time would fit in here, in this place, in this situation as we sit at our plates. Cutlets and potatoes at the Gdańsk shipyard gates surely calls for Armia.

Played loud. Armia's hardcore punk demands to be played at full volume. It doesn't cower, it charges its listeners head-on. And yet I hear wistfulness in the singer's voice, a melancholy violence. As loud as possible without the speakers vibrating off their brackets – that's how I'd like to hear Armia right now. The way they approached Beckett on their album *Triodante*. This music ought to float above the square, echo through the shipyard gates. Armia set Samuel Beckett's 'The Lost Ones' to music, *Le Dépeupleur*, *Wyludniacz*: no space here for sentimentalities.

A monstrous, controlled vehemence. 'From time immemorial rumour has it or better still the notion is abroad that there exists a way out. Those who no longer believe so are not immune from believing so again in accordance with the notion requiring as long as it holds that here all should die but with so gradual and to put it plainly so fluctuant a death as to escape the notice even of a visitor,' Beckett writes about the inmates of his imagined cylinder, in which lost bodies are each seeking their lost one.

Armia make no peace offering. They draw their energy from modernism. Beckett speaks of 'the sedentary' and 'the vanquished'. The sedentary will end up vanquished, 'each in his turn [will] be well and truly vanquished for good and all each frozen in his place and attitude.' You can hear it all the way to Zaspa.

The future is over. We want to go where the shipyard workers live.

Where once the airport stood and today a high-rise housing estate languishes, traversed by a road named after Pope John Paul II and so wide that you immediately see it must be the former runway; there, in one of those barely distinguishable buildings, I could imagine living for a while.

You go ahead and stroll down your restored medieval streets; I can't summon up much enthusiasm for the gables and facades, it all looks almost like it did before our time. You're welcome to stroll and admire away, I don't mind a bit, but let me go to Zaspa.

I don't know whether I'd feel comfortable there; I know nobody, I have difficulties remembering where I have to get off the tram, because all the stops look so similar. I'd like to sit in one of these flats with shoddy doors and presumably thin walls, at a wobbly table with a wax tablecloth, close to the window, the light falling on the armchairs at the back of the room, where my books are. I sit there, thinking for days now about how Joseph Conrad and Georg Trakl almost crossed paths in Kraków at the beginning of the First World War, though the 19th-century writer knew nothing of the 20th-century poet: the Conrad family has just left the city for the safety of the mountains in early October 1914, when Trakl, coming from Galicia, is admitted to the Kraków garrison hospital, where he dies of cocaine poisoning on 3 November, as Conrad is probably on his way home via Vienna and Genoa.

You go ahead, go on looking at the old photos, touched when you see the characters posing by their cars, all vintage models. Touching how proud they are, and their clothes, the beards, hats, hairstyles. As though they'd donned costumes to help their great-grandchildren find their sentimental sides later on. Yet the opposite is true; they dressed in the latest fashions, they took photos of the newest car models as a way of showing their absolute modernity.

Though I don't travel to work, I will board the tram in the mornings and return with the other inhabitants in the evenings. I will walk the concrete runway, walk around car parks and green spaces until I've found my block, and finally also my house number, and then I'll take the lift, if it's working, up to the top floor: home. I will learn my way around some stupid supermarket. I don't know the language, and it will take me a while to work out: *teraz*, Polish: the moment. *Terrasse*, German: a piece of fortified ground outside a house. That dizzy whirl of time and place overlapping across languages.

I will remember how once, one late afternoon in Wrocław, I sat on the *Terasse* outside Witaminka and watched passers-by. The locals, recognisable by the speedy pace of city-dwellers, and the slower tourist groups, herded through a folk-music theme park, fearfully cautious not to get in the way of the two young men doing the rounds of the marketplace, singing and shouting, making circuit after circuit, and stopping outside every restaurant in the hope someone might buy them a beer: two young men born in the late 1980s, revolving around their own axis in a dizzy whirl.

Sometimes I will get off a few tram stops later to view the 'wavy house', as it's called in Gdańsk. I will wait at the traffic lights by McDonald's in the drizzle, cross the road with the stream of pedestrians, and walk the almost-kilometre length of the *falowiec*, the wavy house. While the crowd I'm caught up in dwindles from entrance to entrance, I consider whether there is a link between the building's wave-shaped layout and the 'New Wave', whether I'm walking along a new wave or – the past tense of modernism – an old one. Then the next intersecting street rears into view, a pizzeria on the corner, and I turn around. On the way home, the tram is almost empty. I can find my bearings in my neighbourhood by the monumental mural painted in memory of the first papal visit, raindrops glinting on the varnish of parked cars beneath the streetlamps.

Should I flounder, I will read Zygmunt Haupt and make myself dizzy as I follow his use of tenses. 'Now' meshes with 'always has'; the 'long gone' comes not tomorrow but suddenly in the middle of the night. I cannot discover any nostalgia in there. Zygmunt Haupt, who speaks from the present of things past as though they were two rooms, and he were now sitting in the one with 'past' written on its door.

Somewhere up there, I lean over the edge of a balcony and look towards the sea. One set of neighbours is arguing, the others are quiet. Now and then, at night, I blare out my Armia CDs with the door open to the corridor. Back then, as a child, I discovered time with a slight shudder. I'm still not in search of lost timelessness.

III

'Dear sir. The faiton is finished.' The joy at the arrival of the longed-for news makes its reader blind to the orthographic imprecision, and the narrator's father in Zygmunt Haupt's 'The Wake and the Repast' knows full well what he commissioned from the carriage-maker: a phaeton coach.

The story is set in a hazy early 20th century, in a hazily sketched Podolian snowscape, perhaps because the narrator regards place and time as obvious factors, or perhaps because the sonorous word inspires in him, the boy allowed to accompany his father to the nearest town to collect the luxury vehicle, images that make everything else fade into insignificance.

'And then came Mr Papierski's workshop,' Zygmunt Haupt writes, 'and between wood shavings, sawdust, boards stacked into piles of finished and partly worked material, stood the newborn phaeton; fresh, smelling of varnish, paint, solder, leather straps, patent leather, Manchester velvet and horsehair, with the glint of lantern glass and copper fittings, elastic, with beautifully curved wheels, spokes reflecting the sun, the shells of the hubs, the violin-shaped carriage body and the fine upholstery of the seats, the padded cylinder on the high box – a phaeton.'

Before father and son set out for home, they go for a spin around town to display themselves and their fine carriage to the admiring locals.

If I remember rightly, the first photographs in circulation of the place where the Austrian far-right politician Jörg Haider had a fatal accident on the way from Klagenfurt to his house in Bärental at around one in the morning on 11 October 2008 showed the wreck of his car from behind, whereas later publications preferred the perspective from the front and side. Yet no matter whether the lettering on the car's tail was legible or not – the name of the model immediately did the rounds: Jörg Haider had met his death on his drive through the fog-swathed night in a 'Phaeton'.

A man who opposed a great many things in his life, yet nothing with as much ire and tenacity as contemporary art and literature, died, as I instantly thought on seeing that grotesquely misshapen VW Phaeton, in a car built less than 20 minutes' walk from my home. The glass box on the northern edge of the Grosser Garten calls itself a transparent factory, *Gläserne Manufaktur*, playing on the nearby Meissner porcelain *Manufaktur* and the 'Transparent Man' on display in Dresden's Hygiene Museum.

In the 'transparent factory', paying visitors and those collecting new cars can watch the Phaeton being assembled. Did a car enthusiast, astounded by the silent precision of every step in the VW factory, once flinch for no clear reason as he observed the assembly of the very vehicle later delivered to Jörg Haider?

Dresden. The Grosser Garten. What a place that sends such cars out into the world.

*

The clouds in the sky above Munich were layered so closely that they formed a uniform, graphite-grey, soon cockroach-coloured film. The path from the car park to the museum had led through oil-shimmering puddles, under the projecting roof of the entrance: bicycles, umbrellas, baby buggies. And now I stood with dirty shoes in the mild artificial light, weary of the pictures and the people, my gaze fixed upon a blurred distance, unable to envisage another place I might put myself, surrounded by artworks and in the midst of countless visitors who, like me, had had the idea of spending this rainy early-October Sunday afternoon in the Pinakothek der Moderne. There I stood up on the gallery, wishing myself into a dark world.

No, there was no little patch of yellow wall invented for me by Proust, or Marcel, upon which to fix my gaze, before which I, like an imaginary writer, could have felt faint and collapsed, murmuring 'little patch of yellow wall, little patch of yellow wall'. Seeking, and yet with no destination in mind, I looked down into the open hall from my place on the first floor. Below me, the people steadily peeled out of the ordered crush around the ticket desks and either took the staircase leading up to the art of the 20th century or, and this current seemed broader, turned to the design department on the ground floor, its exhibits seeming to exert a magical attraction on many, even from outside.

My eyes followed them into the exhibition area, past rows of yellow, red and blue chairs arranged against the wall like an installation, and as the visitors dispersed, my attention was caught: an early-model VW Beetle, mounted on scaffolding so as to loom above the observers' heads, protruding into the room as though the immobilised vehicle were falling from the ceiling, deeply dark, painted a matte tone that absorbed the light around it, as though it were falling without ever crashing to the ground.

43

On a day in the early 21st century, in a place dedicated to modernism, I find myself unexpectedly facing a fixed vehicle. As far as I know, the term for this phenomenon is 'stationary traffic'. And perhaps it is not all too abstruse to recall, at this sight, a scene from a novel written 150 years ago; the carriage ride at the beginning of modernism in *Madame Bovary*, in which an afflicted, almost stunned coachman wonders 'what passion for locomotion drove this pair into never wanting to stop.'

We see nothing – that is, we see a landau driving aimlessly around a small French town for half a day, the tired horses, and the witless coachman on his box. We hear of the station, the river, the tow-path, the botanical gardens, the hospital gardens and the harbour, an open field; we read countless names of streets, bridges and quarters. And since they all tell us non-locals very little, the description presents us with no images; all we ever have before us is the carriage, the door, the little window, the drawn yellow linen curtains, where perhaps, if we look closely, something moves; where we can perhaps, if the curtains briefly sway on an uneven stretch of road, make out through a narrow gap something of what is going on in the carriage.

From its interior, a voice calls out: 'Keep going!' or 'No, straight on!' and 'Just keep moving!' Once, a bare hand protrudes from beneath the curtains and scatters scraps of paper on the slight wind. No more than that. And that nothing, of course, inflames us.

Flaubert, who claims to have consistently aimed for moderate temperatures in *Madame Bovary*, works at this juncture with a heated distance, so heated that the scene was suppressed on the novel's first publication – a nothing so obscene that it must disappear. When we are shown nothing but yellow linen curtains, an empty screen, that's when the movie starts up in our minds.

Long after that Munich afternoon, my thoughts kept returning to the old Volkswagen; I could never quite grasp it. That unroadworthy VW had set something in motion.

I couldn't help thinking of the black patches I sometimes see on long autobahn stretches, out of the corner of my eye as I focus on my own lane – images of barely a second, nothing but small dark patches on the hard shoulder, vanishing barely after coming into view, a few square metres of sooty, churned-up, now coarse asphalt; nothing else. It seems to me as if I were seeing them more and more frequently; you might think I'd grown accustomed to them by now, but the same shuddering feeling seizes me every time: a car once burned there, and when the wreckage was removed it left behind a patch of burnt earth, burnt autobahn. Every time anew, I force myself to imagine the driver holding a fire extinguisher, standing in front of the bonnet and aiming into the cloud of heat, or I compel myself, even better, to group firemen in protective suits around the burning vehicle, its passengers poised in the background, obscured by thick smoke, on the other side of the crash barriers, safe.

The kind of mental movies no one wants to see when passing the site of an accident cleared the previous night, the unremarkable traces of a disaster no one remembers, aside from the driver or – always the same fearful question – their relatives. I was reminded of an evening walk my parents took with me when I was perhaps five years old – an odd memory: a family walk by night. The cliffs, the beach, the Baltic not far off, the Laboe memorial to the navy dead visible beyond the Firth of Kiel by day. Perhaps the descent to the beach was dangerous after darkness fell; in the evenings, we kept to the sunken path that began behind our house and led between fields to a gravel pit – but I only knew that from stories.

We were on our way home, hearing the sound of an engine behind us for some time, far away; workers apparently still busy in the gravel pit at night. We had almost reached our building when the noise came closer at top speed. There was no time to take out the front-door key; we leapt off the footpath onto the grass, ran, stopped, turned, and saw a heavy lorry, followed by a patrol car, ramming into a row of cars parked outside the building. It propelled a dark-blue Fiat for several metres ahead of it, then at last the lorry's engine flooded and it came to a standstill not far from us.

Two boys had hot-wired a dump truck in the gravel pit and then failed to find the brakes on their joyride, which became a car chase. A neighbour screamed and wept: 'My little car, my little car.' At the end of their spin, the boys had narrowly missed our VW Beetle, a gift from my grandfather. I see them both next to the policemen on the grass, trembling, apathetic, their eyes feverish. I see flashing blue light, broken glass, oil. Nothing caught fire.

I could see a scene from Mark Twain's *Huckleberry Finn* before me, a book that might have been read to me at bedtime that very year. An incidental scene, a swift glance at a night-time scenario and then the narrative thread is picked up again, that brief flicker forgotten a few lines later. Contrary to their usual habit of sleeping in a hiding place on the riverbank by day and travelling down the Mississippi under cover of darkness, Huck and Jim moor their raft one night near a village and go on land.

They interrupt their journey for an errand; they need food, they want to scout the area. All is sleeping, the two are perhaps already on their way back to the river, and the episode seems almost complete – when the village is all at once bathed in bright light, noise, a jeering crowd, the whole population up and about, a torchlit parade, and in the midst of it, soundless, motionless, a black figure with white patches. From a safe distance, Huck and

Jim watch as the lynch mob leads a horse along the road, on it a man, tarred and feathered. A gallows comes into view – or is it a pyre? – the lights drawing together at one point, and before the reader might see the flames leaping across from the torches to the tarred man, Jim drags Huck away. They run through the underbrush, back to the raft. The two never speak of the scene we just witnessed.

I recently searched the novel for that scene, which I knew only from having it told to me. I began by flicking through and then read all of *Huckleberry Finn*, whose story takes place at around the same time as that of *Madame Bovary*, from beginning to end. And as happens so frequently with passages that stay with the reader so clearly: the scene doesn't exist.

And I thought of my great-grandmother from the Kattowitz region, with its industrial towns extending in all directions, who had been cast up out West in Duisburg and spent most of her life there. Apart from organised excursions to pilgrimage sites and visits to her children – then her grandchildren, then her great-grandchild, me – her move from one steel region to another will have been her only major journey. In Meiderich, she will likely have gone most places on foot, the wide world apparently palpably close by, yet impalpably far away. It could have been a purely imaginary world, had signs of its existence not sometimes physically encroached upon her own life, for instance in the form of a whale that could be seen in a harbour basin for a while, or a monkey my great-grandfather spotted in the cargo hold of a freight ship and brought home from work.

'Oh, come, thou dear infant! Oh come thou with me! For many a game I will play there with thee.' How to drive out the darkness? By making up stories, feverish mind-movies set in the dark. And so my great-grandmother, sharing my bedroom when she visited, recited ballads to me long into the night; her repertoire included nothing edifying or instructive. Quite the opposite: in the stories I remember, the focus was on disturbance, depression, hallucination and death; none released their listener into a bright and orderly world. They were meeting places for mist riders, mountain trolls und woodland sprites. And we have no influence over these creatures' appearance and disappearance; they alone decide on their presence, and rhyme and metre. In fact, the ways in which we tell each other stories about them might only be hapless attempts to persuade us we have these ephemeral creatures under our command. 'I love thee, I'm charm'd by thy beauty, dear boy.'

I knew the long misty days on the north German plains. In the morning I would run to the kitchen window – the world out there was erased. And I had once seen real bog mummies, up close behind glass, black and eyeless with dense, tangled hair and skewed limbs. 'My father, my father, he seizes me fast!'

A voice in the dark. Or a shape staring mutely at us: we hear something without seeing it, the eye perceives something yet the ear doesn't receive the attendant sounds – as soon as our senses fall out of sync, we lose control. 'Dost see not the Erl-King?' We no longer trust ourselves. The ghosts and spirits know that. 'My father, my father, and dost thou not hear / The words that the Erl-King now breathes in mine ear?' And to compensate for the lacking sensation, we hallucinate. All you have to do to teach us to fear is to separate the audio and video tracks.

What use is it that the father talks sense to his child and himself, and speaks of the rising mist, the wind in withering leaves, and the old grey willows, as though he could synchronise the audio and visual tracks in the middle of the film screening? The boy has long since stopped hearing his father.

I thought of the many coachmen and chauffeurs haunting literature and literary history; shifty characters. The carriage driver in Flaubert who refuses to imagine the goings-on behind the yellow curtains – we're unconvinced by such witlessness. The whole town gets the point, as do the readers and even the censors. Of course Flaubert is not Madame Bovary, no matter what he said to the contrary. Instead, the suspicion seems justified that this coachman, an oaf who doesn't understand 'what desire for locomotion drove the pair', is Flaubert himself on the box: Look here, I'm showing you this coach I'm steering around with no destination. Where my language takes you is all your own business. Anyone who thinks the yellow stigma filled up the whole carriage window ought to remember it is merely a linen curtain.

Marcel Proust has his young narrator, the 'little treasure' who would rather be read Flaubert than George Sand, turn into a writer on a ride in an open coach. As a boy, he sits beside the coachman on the box, jotting down his first writings on a prescription pad, unperturbed by the bumpy ride. Writing becomes something, for him, that results from shifts in perspective, the way painting demonstrates: the style, c'est moi.

There he steers his carriage around the world, the implausible narrator, like a coachman on his box or a chauffeur behind his broad windscreen, perceiving his surroundings from constantly changing perspectives – nothing reliable can be expected under such conditions. We are dealing here with helpful spirits who prove to be wayward. They act discreet, willing to serve, they play the invisible servants who hold the reins without putting in any further appearances, just as their clients, their readers, want. And then Flaubert: as an oafish-acting bad coachman, who 'lashed out harder at his two sweat-soaked nags, ignoring the pot-holes, scraping into this and that'.

49

Emma and Léon conceal themselves from prying eyes, seal themselves off from distracting external stimuli. Then Proust lifts the little yellow curtain and lets us watch Swann and Odette 'make Cattleya' on a coach ride. When it comes to himself, though, Proust the writer draws the curtains from Flaubert's scene before his own life, muting all outside stimuli: no distraction, no impression from real life is to disturb his imagination work in the dusky, sound-swallowing room. Of the spectacle on offer outside, at most the scent of petrol may penetrate the curtains on waking in the morning; recollection of his time as an enthusiastic automobilist, when 'the imaginative Agostinelli' knew how to bring out the details of a cathedral portal immersed in darkness with 'supernatural light' by directing car headlamps at the building according to his master's wishes.

Even in his dark world, the writer does not want to do without his chauffeur, who is promptly transformed from a driver to a scribe, making fair copies of his employer's drafts. No, Proust no longer needs to attend the salons to see them in his mind's eye. Everything is present in his memory; the snobs and fops and old aristocracy; the hollow phrases and half-hearted attempts to alleviate the boredom, for instance by introducing a monkey to the group one evening.

Raymond Roussel, the author of *How I Wrote Certain of my Books*, needs neither the sight of that monkey nor the memory of it. Though his *Impressions of Africa* may be the result of a tour of the dark continent, Roussel had himself chauffeured around in a mixture of Flaubert's landau and Proust's isolation cell, without ever once opening the curtain. The blank screen behind which a movie is played: everything based solely on the power of the imagination.

Strange coincidence, then, that Raymond Roussel was betrayed by an actual chauffeur: a man he booked for a trip to

Sicily, who, after Roussel's sudden death in Palermo, drove straight back to Paris to blackmail a nephew of the author, with dubious insinuations. Strange, too, the way this real event seems presaged in Proust: before he collapses in front of the *View of Delft* in the museum, the writer Bergotte, who hasn't written for years, has suffered torturous hallucinations for some time. No longer merely nightmare images or phantasms familiar to insomniacs, but – 'My father, my father, he seizes me fast!' – palpable apparitions, physically felt. They include 'the rage – because Bergotte had murmured in his sleep that he was driving badly – of a raving lunatic of a cabman who flung himself upon the writer, biting and gnawing his fingers.'

That abrupt veer from subservience to tyranny, from familiarity to betrayal. No wonder Odette feels a deep aversion to her lover's coachman. She, an artiste of revealing and concealing, is not willing to rely on the discretion of such a character.

I was reminded of my aunt's, even then, surprising indignation after taking her children to see *Saturday Night Fever*. She was absolutely aghast: people copulating in plain view, on a car bonnet in a parking lot at night. Was that the same year when a pram terrorists pushed into a road made a limousine slam on its brakes? The time when Stammheim-grey plastic shutters appeared everywhere; an unbearable rattle, the slits of light narrowing, and then the room pitch black, not a sound entering from outside. I still haven't seen *Saturday Night Fever*. A pram pushed onto the road, the chauffeur brings the limousine to a halt just in time, and the car is peppered with bullets in the next instant.

And now a child's pram rolls down the steps in Odessa, the White infantry at the top, at the foot of the staircase the mounted Cossacks. The pram rolls past the dead and injured in a hail of bullets, and tips, having reached the end of the stairs, on its side. Neither this pram nor the other carried a baby. And I'm reminded of the always whistle-clean boots; the miserable accuracy; the permanent spitting and polishing and huffing and rubbing of the black leather boots; the ridiculous, frightening cleanliness of certain people who are capable of anything.

Then we saw cars burning night after night in the banlieues of Paris. Every morning, the latest statistics on vehicles ignited in stationary traffic were announced; soon cars outside Greater Paris went up in flame; more places added to the rising, already grotesque arson figures every night; places with names I didn't know – whether Madame Bovary's provincial town was among them, I failed to register.

There were desperate attempts to spot the old symbols in the burning vehicles. Surely symbolism is at play when hundreds of cars burst into flame every night, but symbol interpretation no longer gets a grip on such phenomena, as the stammered reactions and juvenile commentaries revealed. Today I'll set fire to your Renault, tomorrow night you'll burn my Peugeot – the rebellion against power, the building of barricades, the manifest destruction of capitalist symbols? Nothing more than senti-mental memories. The television camera needs bright light? At your service.

I saw myself once again out on the gallery in Munich, the dark VW Beetle dangling in mid-air on the ground floor. My foul mood was directed entirely at that VW; why do they have to taunt me with a car in a museum when I can't avoid the sight of countless cars outside? At last, my eyes disengaged from the exhibit, slid slowly up the hall; opposite, the broad white stripes of the gallery balustrade, and there, a painting on the wall. From my perspective, it looked as though this triptych and the Volkswagen were on the same vertical axis, as though they were meant to be linked in some way. As though they'd been placed, for the observer from the first-floor gallery, in a delicate balance.

I approached the painting, clearly recognisable from a distance as a piece by Francis Bacon, rendered in shades of red as if in contrast to the November-coloured car. In the top half, a monochrome, luminous red wall extends almost to the left edge. Beneath it, occupying the entire width of the triptych, a green-tinged, red-grey floor. At the top left, in an open passage leading into darkness, a female figure, apparently turning to face the scene that opens up before us. It's possible the naked woman is eyeing the two men in dark suits and white hats visible on the right-hand wing, or that they are watching the woman without her noticing. Bacon's figures' gazes can never be clearly determined; you never know whether his faces, his bodies move of their own accord or whether they are shaped by external pressure, the way you could also never say whether Francis Bacon is portraying pain in his paintings, or whether these pictures *are* that pain.

With Francis Bacon, I can't help compulsively searching for the eyes, and here, too, in the 1965 triptych entitled *Crucifixion* in front of me now. The central manifestation on the left-hand wing: a fleshy arm, a dog, a skull as if bedded on mattresses, red, pink, white. The middle part: from an apparatus stretching upwards, perhaps a home furnishing, hangs something like a human, the upper body resting on the floor. Above it, a second creature seems to be pushing its way into the opened body; an animal, a comic character. And on the right wing, where the two gents are leaning against a table, a man on the outer edge, turned in on himself, looking down, perhaps standing on a mat, perhaps eyeing a turquoise liquid, perhaps that's his shadow.

Because the back of his head is so clear, his ear, his neatly combed-back hair, my search for his eyes fell flat, and I grasped at other pale round spots appearing in the pale-pink surroundings: there, that white circle on a red background on the bare upper arm. As I went closer, I spotted a swastika shimmering through the titanium white.

Now the images raced back and forth between Bacon's *Crucifixion* and the VW Beetle: Didn't I once see a sheet of paper on which the painter and 'despatch runner' they called the Führer had scribbled a first draft of the 'Strength through Joy' car? Has he managed, if not with his kitschy paintings but with the manifestation of his mobility fantasy, to be exhibited in a museum of modernism at the beginning of the third millennium, here in Munich, the former 'City of the Movement'? And has National Socialism, which competed with socialism on so many matters, thus achieved one of their ruthless common goals, long after the movement's own demise: to blur the differences between art and crafts – no matter the expense, no matter how many human lives it cost to equate zealous crafts with obstinate art? Who wipes the spilled brains from the leather tips before the SS boots find their place in an illuminated display cabinet, as a historical document of German design art?

The naked, oppressed people and their oppressors in Bacon's pictures; the open, pulsing, stinking flesh, the fresh blood and the scabbed wounds; all the slaughterhouse waste of the 20th century that Francis Bacon seems to spread before us – and the lovingly preserved VW with not a splash of dirt on its sparkling chrome. A word like 'silencer', a word like 'clutch', a word like 'boot'. In the Pinakothek der Moderne, I found the sight of a VW Beetle obscene.

After a while – I'd done some swearing and cursing on the gallery; the poor friends who'd come to the museum with me – I calmed down, regained some distance, a heated distance, and began to doubt: was I not at risk myself of appropriating

Francis Bacon's paintings to serve my own ends? Of course, people asked the painter about the swastika armband. No, the historical significance of the symbol was not the main thing, Francis Bacon said in conversation. He had indeed been inspired by a photograph showing Hitler with other Nazis, but the image had merely provided a solution to a problem: at exactly that spot, that flesh-coloured part, he needed an additional patch of colour, a red accent around the arm, for aesthetic reasons. Thus, Bacon was not motivated by a wish to load his triptych with meaning by making use of a familiar political symbol universally known to this day. That doesn't defuse his work. In my eyes, Bacon's background statement makes his painting all the more unsettling.

Smouldering carriage curtain, inflamed little patch of wall. Feathers against a black backdrop – a human figure in torchlight. No, the scraps of paper thrown by a bare hand from the carriage window, as they 'scattered in the wind, and farther off lighted like white butterflies on a field of red clover all in bloom'. Or an insignificant white patch on a red background. Where is language leading me, where are we drifting? Is the writer a hallucinating boy, a calm-coaxing rider and a whispering Erl-King all at once?

During my work on this piece, which appears to have lost its original title – 'Early Film' – along the way and might now better be called 'The Necessity of Sleep', or simply 'October, November, December' – during the days I spent reading, walking around my flat and constantly taking notes, it occurred to me at some point to look again in W. G. Sebald to see how he moves, in a talk, from the image of the network of lights above the administrative complex of the Daimler corporation in Stuttgart, to an image of the convoys of lorries bearing the Mercedes emblem in zones of devastation around the world.

I wanted to know specifically, in detail, how he structures his sentences, which conjunctions he uses, how he lets image flow into image without ever submitting to a corset of justifications, without having to make argumentative inferences, without utilising the unsatisfactory means of drawing an express conclusion from his observations, which makes everything disappear again at the end. Reading and rereading that one sentence, I didn't find out. Instead, it occurred to me that the Stuttgart speech was his last piece of writing – a few days later, W. G. Sebald died in a car accident.

And I was reminded of my grandfather, who was run over outside his own front door on a rainy autumn or winter night in the early 1970s. Returned late from work, he had parked his car on the opposite side of the road and stepped out onto the street, glinting black in the drizzle or heavy fog, when he was hit by a speeding car.

My grandmother opened the door; perhaps he'd left his key at the office. She hadn't noticed that all the doorbells in the building had rung. In front of her a young man, pale in the face and trembling, the young woman beside him barely capable of speaking, and my grandmother understood just enough to go to the telephone and dial the emergency number.

Someone was lying on the edge of the road, a paramedic bent over him, the whole neighbourhood standing outside the house, the ambulance there, the police, and my grandmother was still peering down the road to see if the familiar car was coming; my grandfather ought to have been there ages ago.

At last, the ambulance workers lifted the injured man carefully onto the stretcher. From his briefcase, presumably opened in the hope of clues to the accident victim's identity, a sandwich box fell to the ground. Hit the pavement, a dull sound, the plastic box empty; my grandmother knew that sound. And at that moment, she realised who the stranger was who had been run over outside her front door.

Now I wanted to know precisely how many days had passed between W. G. Sebald's Stuttgart speech and his fatal accident. I remembered I'd heard the news on a Sunday; I was on a slow train, 'in the Holstein plain with an unbreakable sky and, north of Flensburg, the wood-coloured cows on the gentle slopes of Denmark,' in the words of the Spanish writer Juan Benet, who is still completely unknown in both German and English. Expecting nothing in particular, I flicked through the Sunday papers, surrounded by country youths and tired drinkers. When I saw the photograph of Sebald with his arms crossed, leaning into a corner, the rough brick wall, the grey patches of plaster and, not easy to make out in the black-and-white shot, flecks of saltpetre, lichen or mould, I thought at first of an illustration for a new essay, perhaps a laudation. I began to read: 'He died at the wheel of his car on Friday evening.' Movies no one would want to see, in my mind. Yet from the realm of language comes the echo: 'And if thou'rt unwilling, then force I'll employ.'

I took the obituaries out of their folder, counted back from Sunday, 16 December 2001 to the previous Friday, and noted – eerie where language can lead us: the date on which I would present this piece was the fourth anniversary of W. G. Sebald's death.

'... and finally the precious substance of the tiny patch of yellow wall. His giddiness increased; he fixed his eyes, like a child on a yellow butterfly which he is trying to catch, upon the precious patch of wall. "This is how I ought to have written," he said. "My last books are too dry. I ought to have gone over them with several coats of paint."' – How delightful, Bergotte, to think this in the form of a detail of the *View of*

57

Delft that exists solely in language. – 'He repeated to himself, "Little patch of yellow wall, with a sloping roof, little patch of yellow wall." While doing so he sank down upon a circular divan. And then at once he ceased to think that his life was in jeopardy and, reverting to his natural optimism, told himself: "It is just an ordinary indigestion from those potatoes; they weren't properly cooked; it is nothing."' – Nothing more, Francis Bacon, than a red patch that must be painted on a figure's bare upper arm. – 'A fresh attack beat him down: he rolled from the divan to the floor, as visitors and attendants came hurrying to his assistance. He was dead. Permanently dead? Who shall say?'

*

On the way back from a day trip to Poland we stopped again in Jelenia Góra, previously called Hirschberg, to eat something before we crossed the border. We parked on a cleared site on the edge of the old town, where children gathered around our car; it seemed there weren't many tourists there at that time. An early autumn evening, the sun would soon be setting; we walked over the hill in the soft light, joining the stream of pedestrians, shoppers, after-work strollers, families on their way to evening prayers.

Once we'd seen enough of the medieval alleys and it had turned dark, with hardly anyone on the streets but us, we decided on one of the restaurants beneath the arcades on the market square. I don't remember what it was called, why we picked that particular one – perhaps the promise of traditional dishes, the curtains in the windows, no radio playing inside, and we still had a good way to go through the night. In that restaurant in the southern Polish town of Jelenia Góra, I saw for the first time in my life – and, if I don't return there, presumably also for the last time – a copy of a Pieter Claesz still life.

A largely unknown 17th-century Dutch master, a name meaningful only to still-life specialists. Certainly not an obvious choice for the copyist, perhaps an artist or a hobbyist, a lifelong amateur who suddenly – on what impulse? – breaks out of his routine and feels the need to copy, instead of a Rembrandt or a van Gogh, a painting showing nothing more than a table laid with a bread roll, a large glass and a pewter plate.

A single table inside the restaurant was occupied; two couples in their mid-fifties who had already finished their meal. I can't remember whether they spoke Polish, though I do know their conversation was heated as they waited for the waitress to arrive with coffee and cognac. We sat down at the next table, a red linen tablecloth, plastic placemats with folkloric motifs, a small vase with an artificial flower in the middle, a salt shaker, pepper.

With the other guests' coffee, the attentive waitress brought us an ashtray and two of those slightly sticky, rarely used menus, in English. Every time we turn a page it makes a repulsive sound; the writing has come away from the paper in places and is stuck to the inside of the protective sheath. What I ordered I don't recall; some kind of local speciality. The English wasn't much help to me – the waitress spoke to us in German, and food can't be translated.

She disappeared to the kitchen, and I looked over at the bar; a man polishing glasses. We could tell the restaurant had been renovated not long ago – a place that had once had character, albeit not necessarily a particularly good character. Now the old stuffiness had been replaced by cleanliness, brown carpeting, the walls an indefinable beige, practical, cosy, nicotine-repelling. And then I saw the Pieter Claesz.

That is, to begin with, there was something familiar on the wall, which I barely perceived at first as a still life by that painter, perhaps not even as a painting. A rectangle blending into the unfamiliar surroundings; the calm seeming to belong only here, in this restaurant on the market place in Hirschberg. At the same time, however, something in me was touched; the sight of it stood out from what was around it. That table on the right – it is there on the edge of almost every Claesz – and the angle of light – the light always falls from the left – and the reflection of the light in the large glass – a Berkemeyer or a Römer, Claesz painted their shapes over and over, sometimes using the same glasses for years – and the rough surface of a white bread roll straight from the oven in relation to the reflection from the cool, smooth pewter plate – Pieter Claesz painted bread rolls and metal objects all his life.

It was nothing unfamiliar in this soon-empty restaurant with its air of post-communist tristesse, quite the opposite: the space the picture let me look into was a space I knew well. The world of Pieter Claesz – in Jelenia Góra, sat before a huge plate of meat, fried potatoes and raw vegetables, I first understood it as part of my own world.

Unlike his contemporary Snijders, for instance, Pieter Claesz from Haarlem never painted large kitchen still lives with game, let alone a living stag – the *jelen* in the town's name, the *Hirsch* in the German version. Nor are there any landscapes by him, not a single hill – *Berg*, *góra* – and no people sitting at table to eat game stew or pickled herring with caper berries. He had no particular interest in bouquets or insects. Only one picture of his has a cat, sitting sideways on the table, its fur rough. Cats were not his forte. Perhaps someone else painted that.

People only appear in Claesz's work in the form of skulls; death is the end of things, the skull an object that reminds us

60

of ourselves. In one of his vanitas still lives, Pieter Claesz concealed a self-portrait, a figure reflected in a glass sphere, sitting at an easel, his eyes fixed on the very table before us. In either morning or evening light. The mirror image of a bearded man in a hat, holding a brush and staring at a skull: the painter himself, whom we watch almost unnoticed at work, as refracted light. When night comes, he will vanish like the observed, painted objects, into darkness.

Ultimately, Claesz did not capture objects in his still lives, nor their differing surface structures. Instead, Pieter Claesz studied light conditions. He painted light as it fell through the window of his studio and made things appear.

From my seat, I couldn't see all the details of the Claesz copy, there on the dull yellow wall, in semi-darkness on the way between the kitchen and the toilets. Perhaps, though, the picture was ideally hung in such dusky light, in that musty imitation of cosiness. Instantly visible to every visitor and yet concealed, the way Claesz's works must have hung in Haarlem's bourgeois homes during his lifetime, in the houses of rich grocers, brewery-owners, in establishments like this one, narrow, cramped, the walls seeming damp and the bedlinen clammy, should you have to ask for a room for the night.

The closer I got to the picture, the vaguer and more blurred it became; I could only tell it was a copy after Pieter Claesz from a distance – the composition, the use of browns, white lead, black, the restrained urgency. The still life, as far as I recall, was signed – a copyist who signs his own initials, how strange – and dated 1991. How had the painter come across his source?

He appeared to have copied a poor-quality postcard. The Hirschberg copyist won't have sat before an original – and if so, he had to have been short-sighted and picked up on nothing of Claesz's subtleties. The shell of a walnut as distinct from its core. The pickled herring and its shimmer. The grape beside the wild

61

strawberry. The cut surfaces of a halved orange, the way they contrast its peel, and on the other side the porcelain dish with boiled prawns, their armour winking pink and white. In Claesz, everything depends on such details, which distinguish him from his imitators, from his students; but his admirer from Jelenia Góra might just as well – if those details were not important to him – have turned to any other Dutch still life from the early 17th century.

No, the Claesz copyist, whom the landlord will have commissioned to kit out his newly renovated restaurant with oil paintings, can hardly have worked from an original in 1991, that much is clear. In museums, Pieter Claesz's still lives have always been hung in hidden spots, inconspicuous in some nook, if not stored in the depot. For many years, he was referred to only as 'Monogrammist PC', 'Master PC' – after the painter's death, his name was soon lost along with him, and then to a certain extent his work. The experts no longer considered themselves capable of identifying it; the pictures were attributed to other artists or simply moved out of view. Pieter Claesz's first-ever solo exhibitions started in November 2004, when he had been dead for almost 450 years, in Haarlem, in Zurich, in Washington, far from the northern foothills of the Karkonosze, far from Jelenia Góra.

Had this Claesz work been part of a regularly rotated set of calendar images in Poland, posters available from state art traders to decorate living-room walls? A handful of reproductions, chosen by unclear figures under unclear aspects, for the edification of the citizenry. A series of European masterpieces, compiled slightly differently in each country. In retrospect, no one could say why these particular pictures found their way into their households. In East Germany, for instance, there were van Gogh's sunflowers, which I discovered on the parlour wall of an agricultural conglomerate near Stralsund in the early 1990s

– everyone but me knew them; there was not a great deal of choice for people wanting to embellish their homes. Was this still life, then, a Polish standard picture, a basic for every second mock-historic restaurant on the market square, beneath the arcades? Except that our restaurant-owner had wanted something better, a real oil painting instead of the print on display everywhere else?

Or had Pieter Claesz always had a following of Polish admirers, semi-clandestine? Had connoisseurs always been exchanging art prints of his monochrome breakfast pieces, swapping souvenir postcards from Amsterdam for a large-format misprint from a Hungarian book of still lives? Perhaps the Hirschberg copyist whose signature I could not decipher is a member of such a tenebrous alliance, admirers of the covert Haarlem master and his friendly consistency, his restrained inexorability, I puzzled, back in the car, as we drove through the Polish night to the border.

*

Lessing's painted fire screen. Perhaps, driven by puerile cruelty, they only intend to enjoy watching the tortured creature die, or perhaps the sounds of torment most likely accompanying the spectacle – which I imagine as ear-splitting screeches emitted at no other instant than that of a living being's most extreme fear, coupled with the scent of scorched fur and the desperate motions, weakening gradually above the flame, of the small body becoming aware of its powerlessness – have made for an unexpected show with which the animal sweetens their appetite: with their wide eyes, and deep furrows around their open mouths, the two children, their faces lifted out of darkness by the campfire over which they are leaning so curiously as they roast a rat, thus by no means corresponding to the usual depiction of innocent children – with their ugly features, they look as though their pastime, previously little different to other games of luring and catching an animal only to have crossed a hitherto accepted boundary through the subsequent steps of skewering and adjusting a domestic or agricultural pest over an open fire, had all at once, in view of the dying creature, cast them back as if by magic into their own creatureliness.

There can be no doubt that animals, like humans, have an image of death that flashes before them in moments of fear for their lives, which can be read in the behaviour or facial expression of numerous species. The individual's fear for their own existence: an impulse in which humans and animals equate to one another, in which humans, when seeing it in an animal, must therefore recognise themselves. The wild stare, as if the children were veering between horror and obsession as they wait to see whether the rat has taken its last breath or whether one very last inhalation might follow, as if they instinctively grasped what they are capable of, and as though they did not grasp it either.

Among the few mainly vague images, as if emerging from darkness, that I associate with Gotthold Ephraim Lessing, this one, two children roasting a rat, is the clearest, perhaps because it needs no words to explain it. An image I came across many years ago – on grimy spring days shot through with scant green – on a visit to Lessing's house in Wolfenbüttel, and that has occurred to me again and again since I first entered those rooms, though I could not say whether Lessing ever saw it himself. Its involuntary presence, however, edges all other questions into the background, for instance whether that fire screen depicting the two children at the campfire was in front of the open fireplace in Lessing's day, and whether Lessing – if the fire screen did not in fact come into the house at a later date – really spent time in that room during his Wolfenbüttel years.

It may well be that Lessing knew nothing of these children, this rat, this campfire – the questions are irrelevant to me in view of the mental image of him sitting on winter days, once darkness has fallen, precisely there by the fireplace and, wanting to look into the fire for a while, seeing not logs and embers but this picture of a fire concealing the real fireplace. For even if Lessing had sat before this fire screen – mulling the last words of a manuscript from which he looks up, or exhausted by a conversation lasting most of the evening – he must not necessarily have consciously perceived what it depicted; the children may have remained concealed from him, either because he did not focus on them, with eyes tired from reading, or because little of the depiction was recognisable since the glow from the fireplace placed the opaque screen in a glowing red frame before which the oil painting sank into darkness.

I experienced for myself that people can see this picture of the rat-roasting in broad daylight and not be aware of it, despite its odd and drastic nature, because I was not alone on my visit but rather spent several hours in that very room with a larger group, during which no one else noticed the fire screen, and even among those who frequent the house on a daily basis to maintain the memory of everything related to Lessing and his life there, it was impossible for me to find anyone who had ever paid close attention to the picture or could give me any information about it. Little by little, the picture thus detached itself from its possible historical background, and in the end I was glad not to have found out anything about the fire screen, for those very discoveries we think we have been the first to make, even though they would have been in equally easy reach of anyone else, embed themselves all the deeper in ourselves;

we believe ourselves to be 'in the loneliest depth of that forest, where I have listened to many a speaking animal'. Discoveries like these become visions, which we command according to our own imaginings; embellishing and reshaping the original source over time, to which no one could raise an objection, the fire screen becoming a piece of private property in the mind's eye, unaltered by the fact that I am using a borrowed style to describe it.

The fire, the light. And its reverse, an iron plate decorated with a scenario and carried by four feet, which holds back sparks from the fireplace and thus keeps the house from burning down. As though the room were wilderness itself, as dark and mysterious and uncharted, in which the fire lit by human hand embodies human civilization with its bright glow. The rat was still squirming in its death struggle just moments ago. No bloodcurdling screech to be heard now. The roasted flesh is no longer on the skewer. The shimmer which emphasised the children's contorted features is growing ever weaker; at some point the last ember fizzles out, and now someone stares only at a dark surface in the darkness. The frenzy, and the astonishment at their own frenzy, have vanished from view. 'I meditated, I chose, I rejected, my brow glowing,' Lessing writes where he speaks of the forest of speaking animals, and just as we might be left, after reading his *Treatises on Fables*, with the impression that questions of ethics and morals and the reader's ability to draw their own conclusions – whereby the author focuses on children – were no more important than those of syntax and the correct use of animals; on the contrary, we might think anyone who had clarified for themselves in which type of sentences they make which kinds of animals appear had already gained a great deal, and the moral would then arise of its own accord with no need to be expressly formulated, so we might equally think, on mention of a glowing brow in a prominent place, that writing meant nothing other than someone turning to a hot fire screen and finally touching it despite all their inner resistance, so as to lean over a painted campfire with two children and be close to that rat as it dies in horrific torment.

IV

With foreboding, I'd breathed the cold air by the Wannsee and got in the car towards eight in the evening. Snowfall, which would have complicated matters for the moment but brought great relief in the bigger picture, wasn't to be expected that night; instead, everything indicated temperatures far below freezing. Over the course of my drive beneath the starry sky, isolated banks of fog around the lake and then on the ring road were to transform into a hard landscape of frost.

If I'd had a passenger, they would have already noticed my disquiet on the way there that noon, when I set off for Berlin in the winter sunlight, through the landscape growing ever sandier to the north, marked by ever more pine forests, past places with eye-catching names such as Ortrand, Freienhufen, Calau or Märkisch Buchholz along the pleasantly driveable, mainly empty autobahn, its repairs now almost completed after almost a decade. Unlike on previous drives, I could enjoy neither the view of my surroundings nor the road ahead, soothing the eye in its even shade of grey. I was distracted, listening not to my inner voice but to the car's, which was making unfamiliar sounds, quiet to start with, as though metal were knocking against metal at a great distance, alternating between rhythmic and then unmeasured rattling or rumbling, which I blamed first on the road surface and the cassettes roughly piled in the glove compartment, then on the not-properly closed bonnet, only to admit at last that it must be coming from the engine bay. At one point on the outbound drive, as though listening carefully affected my vision, I'd even almost veered off the road.

That night, the gentle knocking sounds had soon become an unceasing din, so loud and frightening that I – with no passenger to talk to and perhaps figure out the disturbance with – kept turning up the radio, to drown in familiar noise that indicated nothing unusual. The knocking, however, spread to the whole of the car; I felt it in my feet, my right arm, my shoulders, and I was alone. I sped along the autobahn.

Now I was sitting at a plastic table and waiting for the breakdown service, counting and calculating and smoking. Outside, the petrol station, otherwise no light far and wide; I had ended up in Brandenburg's nowhere. I counted the time, the kilometres; neon light above the petrol pumps, I saw myself in the window pane, dishevelled, wild-eyed. An afterimage: the rosy shimmer on the car ceiling above me from the rear lights of the van ahead, vanishing into the night. From behind come new lines, white light encroaching upon the matte fabric, a lorry that I recently drove past gaining ground. It won't be able to overtake me here, alongside a building site. It will shunt me along, full beam; there's nowhere to get out of its way. Then an exit, and I toiled my way to the service station at 40 km/h before my car's engine died. I'd driven as fast as I could, the worst possible decision, as I would later find out; that is, I'd tried to drive fast, but no matter how hard I put my foot down, the car had only ever slowed, and by the time I got to Zossen it was clear the 200 kilometres from Berlin to Dresden would take me at least five hours, if I managed them at all that late-November Sunday night.

While I studied the artificial floral arrangement in its pot, the same things kept revolving around my mind. The blossom was an odd work of crepe, shaped by who knows whom, who knows where; an Asian fantasy flower created out of paper, or perhaps the recreation of a natural blossom after all, which I, anything but an expert on flower names, was unable to place. What if my car had some major damage that couldn't be repaired on the fly? The breakdown service could tow me to the nearest town, but I couldn't say whether that would be of any use. I would have to stay overnight, but is there a hotel in this part of the world, where not even a house is visible? As with every time I'm confronted with artificial flowers, here too I raised the decorative pot to my nose to make sure that paper flowers really don't smell. Like an insect, I always let the colour show me the way at first. What will become of my plans for tomorrow, what if my car has taken its very last drive and there's no getting away from this service station? I could sit here for an unspecified length of time, might have to – or ask one of the people here whether they'd give me a lift. But where to?

I've always been bad at describing colours; the correct name seemed to be doll's skin or high-blood-pressure pink, or hibiscus, if that's a colour, and aside from that, it wasn't easy to determine the colour under the artificial light. I was in Rüblingsheide, someone had told me, near Duben, but those names meant nothing to me, on closer inspection. Daylight would never reach the arrangement, however; in spaces like this bistro, daylight fights in vain against the artificial lighting. Magenta. Antique pink, possibly. I certainly wouldn't be asking the five figures in their mid-twenties perched on stools around the table on the way to the toilets, the only guests beside myself. There would have been no point; their car, if they even intended moving on that night, would already be full. The flowers – perhaps cabbage rose or gerbera, or at least that's what their colour suggested to me – did smell, of course; I was overcome by a slight unease, and what use would it have done to ask the staff here, the cook, the cashier and cleaner, the man at the newspaper stand or the petrol pump attendant. They couldn't leave, they had work to do. And no one else was here.

Somewhere between Berlin and Dresden was a place where drivers left the known world as soon as they made the mistake of stopping their car at night. It's possible the blossoms had lost their original colouring – that happens quickly. It's possible these jungles of wire and crepe paper on every table, in which the blossoms looked rather randomly placed, had their heyday long behind them and had faded. The large yellow, always dusty-looking leaves trembled, and, as if instinctively, I removed my hands from the tabletop – I had the feeling my whole body was shaking, and I thought my trembling had transferred to the reeds, as if we were somehow connected.

I took a book out of my bag, still firmly believing I could convince myself my stay here differed in no way from the kind of breaks I usually take during long drives. I opened the volume, looked at the letters but did not read. Before my mind's eye floated an unclear impression of mineral oil, which I always imagine to be dark, black and heavy. Though it is incorrect; that image of an opaque, barely liquid mass persists so stubbornly because we very rarely see mineral oil, and then only briefly. Who looks closely when they top up the oil in their engine, who remembers anything of overflowed diesel once the van has been refuelled and returned to the car hire company? That iridescent web in all shades of the rainbow, however, that we admired as children on top of a puddle and divided with the tip of a Wellington or a stick, only to see it merging the next instant into new shapes and patterns, we would never link as adults with the mundane fuel that propels our cars. In fact, diesel and petrol are pale, clear liquids with a slight tinge of yellow, almost raspberry.

From the rattling speakers in the ceiling cladding came music now – I knew the song, I'd first heard it perhaps 20 years ago; 'Red Red Wine'. I could have sung along; my voice would not have been noticeable in sync with the singer's so unobtrusively thin vocals here on the radio. I looked into the picture spread before me in the window pane; the hydroculture-topped planter right behind me, the bulky yet frail rack on wheels where we were supposed to take our trays of used crockery, behind that the so-called Fresh Centre, a line of now barely filled salad bowls beneath a glass cover, on which countless weary travellers had left a fine shimmer of forehead grease, and then the left edge of the self-service counter, which melded into the cash-desk area with its space for resting trays and a raised stool. I peered around in the picture; the group of men at the table were still talking, getting slightly louder in fact as though to drown out the song. The cook was staring into space – I could tell he wasn't registering the music; his hand lay motionless on the glass cover, not even his forefinger tapping along mechanically, the heating element glowing slightly and bathing the last schnitzel in warm light.

The cashier was not in her place, perhaps cleaning the floor of the ladies' toilet for the second time since I'd arrived, or perhaps she had to be alone to listen to music and would retreat from the bistro zone into the tiled area whenever she liked a song on the radio. The mirrored wall, the clear white, the glittering stainless-steel fittings, and her, mop in hand, perfectly still while the music emanated from the concealed speakers, a plastic bucket on the floor and alongside it, unmoving, two pale slip-on shoes. I didn't want to disturb her.

75

But the gents' table, it seemed, could have used some cheering up. One of the two young men who, if I heard rightly, were speaking Czech and might not be able to follow the three Germans' chatter, had been looking rather down for some time now, as if not quite sure his friends weren't discussing a plan in their language to cheat the two others at the table in a deal, perhaps to do with used cars that had to be taken across the border that night, or even got rid of for good. For two rounds, he'd only sporadically sipped at his beer and stared into the flower arrangement by his glass, like me. He was the driver, to be sure, and his concerns were absolutely unfounded, as it turned out the next moment when one of his friends, the loudest, called over to the food counter and asked, albeit perhaps in rather a coarse tone, for a hot chocolate for the young man, whose eyes now briefly met mine in the window. A friendly pat on the back, accompanied by a word I didn't understand, and he turned back to his table-fellow, who fetched him back into their midst with an almost caring extra nod. No, the driver had no reason to hang his head that late Sunday evening in no-man's land; his friends cared about him, they clinked their glasses to him, raised them high in the air and drank deeply, and called for cocoa again a moment later.

The cook, however, clearly had no great taste for such declarations of friendship, retorting that the hot chocolate – probably powder stirred into hot water and frothed up – was already made, waiting at the till, but someone from the gents' table would have to bother to fetch the mug. It's possible he had no friends like these and longed to spend an evening in lively chat instead of alone behind his counter of congealing food, or maybe he'd been exhausted when he started his shift, which perhaps had only just begun and wouldn't end until after sunrise, an eternity if you're looking ahead to eight or ten hours shackled to this place while the travellers are allowed to move on, invigorated, after refreshments – in any case, he wasn't prepared to make an exception to the strict law of self-service and serve one of his guests a hot drink at their table.

I would have liked to leap up and take the mug of cocoa to the table now, firstly to do the young men a favour and thus perhaps get talking to them, and secondly to appease the cook, who seemed not only to be in a bad mood due to some past event, but also to fear trouble if the small, actually harmless group intended to spend the rest of the night drinking beer here, as if he were imagining a fight or already thinking about how to drag four men the next morning, dead drunk, sleepy and heavy, into a dark room behind the kitchen where cleaning equipment, flour and road salt were kept.

That's when the man from the breakdown service tapped me on the shoulder. For a second I was torn; I gathered up my belongings, quickly deposited my half-empty coffee cup on the rack and wanted to follow the mechanic in pale overalls outside as soon as possible, yet at the same time something held me back, perhaps because the hour-long wait I was told on the telephone to expect had not yet expired, perhaps because I couldn't take my leave from this place so surprisedly. In my haste, I left the building without a word. I don't think anyone turned to see me leave. The radio was probably playing another news bulletin, oldies and the same ads over and over, one of them – strange at that time of night – inviting us to visit Kamenz Upholstery Heaven, with no obligations. The mechanic was waiting by my car, the only one in the car park aside from the one with the Czech licence plate. It was cold, no more music, I was back in the Brandenburg night.

The young man shone a light into the engine bay and spoke. I didn't listen properly, breathing the winter air; he bent wires into shape and sprayed something on the contacts, and before he could assure me I would manage the rest of my way home,

I noticed all weight falling from my shoulders. Forgotten, that noise as if the engine were about to explode at any moment; forgotten, the stretch of autobahn I was still in, with building sites and no hard shoulder; forgotten, even, that the young man at the newspaper and confectionary stand, who had later disappeared into an office and not come out again, had initially refused to let me use the telephone and had pointed at the coin-operated booths at the entrance, yet refused to change a note; forgotten that eventually, a woman's voice in the receiver merely informed me repeatedly that the number I'd dialled couldn't be reached from this telephone; forgotten that I ran out to the petrol pumps in my desperation, to find someone who might lend me their telephone; forgotten at last too, how embarrassing it was when the pump attendant, apparently the operator of the service station, took me back inside and instructed the stand-in cashier or apprentice to put me in touch with the breakdown service via the in-house telephone. And hadn't I long wished to spend more time at one of these motorway service stations than it takes to pay for petrol or buy a drink? Hadn't I always imagined being in this situation would be exciting, circumstances allowing me to breathe in the scent of cleaning fluids in peace, listen to night-time radio and inspect the artificial flowers for a while?

I get in the car, I start the engine, then I'm back on the autobahn. I've made a mental note not to drive faster than 80 kilometres an hour; now, in the first winter's night – or so I cobble together the technical explanations – at high speed, the incoming wind cools the engine too much to run smoothly. If the rattling and halting begins anew, I'm to take a short break in a car park so the engine can warm up again. The radio stays off, I smoke, and the man from the breakdown service overtakes me just before the turn-off for Dresden and gives a friendly flash of his lights into the night before he drives on towards Cottbus.

And so I cruise along until a brightly lit industrial complex appears on my left, Schwarzheide. Crude oil, there's that dark, heavy crude oil as well, of course, I realise now – how could I have forgotten that the fine, refined forms clearly differ from heavy oil? And then the stutter is back, just a touch, but I don't want to take the risk, and I turn into a motorway car park at the next opportunity. I wait, but without impatience, possessed by an unimagined calm, feeling like a new man. It's not much farther to home. The engine just needs a break. I get out, not a single car passing at this time of night; I'm alone, Schwarzheide behind me, the Sorbian Schornegosda, radiating in the night for no one but me. On the other side, above open fields, the starry sky.

Little by little the dots pale, some already vanishing, and I see the deep blue shade of the sky in the east soon threaded through with a reddish shimmer. Not much longer and the sun will rise – the new day is here. I haven't slept a wink, haven't washed; I extinguish my cigarette on the tarmac, stretch and leap in one bound over the crash barrier dividing the car park from the field. Fresh and invigorated, I head into the morning.

*

Hell is other people's heaven. In hell – in my hell – songs play all day that mention the colour red: UB40's version of 'Red Red Wine', for instance, or 'Lady in Red' by Chris de Burgh. In the dormitory, the endless long corridors, in the lift, in the spa area, even on the so-called quiet terrace: Everywhere, the air is filled with these two songs. When one ends, the other begins, over and over. 'Music? I hadn't noticed,' people will tell me, or: 'What's your problem with it, Marcel? It's nice.' In my hell, people will be consistently over-familiar. Prince's 'Little

Red Corvette' won't be part of the repertoire; there's no room for ambiguities in my hell.

*

On my drives between Dresden and Berlin, I've seen a hotel out of the corner of my eye countless times since 1996; a red box of a building surrounded by pine and birch forest bordering directly on the autobahn, not far from the Schwarzheide exit. More seldomly on the way out in the morning, but every time on the drive back at night. How frequently the hotel's name has changed over the years, I don't know, but it has always retained the same charisma. A place for fantasies. You could make an espionage film here. Or a gruesome murder mystery. And you wouldn't even need a corpse.

*

I was wide awake at just after seven, matte light outside the window, before the sun appeared over the horizon, over the park; an oval, orange-coloured sun. It vanished in a layer of cloud, high fog, smog, then reappeared, pallid yellow, and now it's dazzling while I – at quarter past eight – sit up here on the 16th floor in the breakfast room of the Hotel Express in Kiev.

There is a sour smell from the buffet. The television is on and I'm getting tired again already, the television voices making me switch off mentally. A news channel, first advertising, then football, then a speech by Vladimir Putin; I understand no more than that. Outside, a haze over the city; it forms as the sunlight grows stronger. Waking up – but waking up *whereto*? Into this world of the breakfast room, into the world of the novel I'm working on, into the city world of Kiev around me?

At 8:35 it's as though a switch has been flicked. Having just thought, 'This terrible Nescafé,' I'm now glad when a young waiter serves me coffee and brings me an ashtray. At the same moment, it no longer annoys me that all other breakfast guests have appeared in slippers or Adidas flipflops.

The television is now showing images of the 'Orange Revolution', but I can't judge whether it's archival footage or celebrations to mark the now, in November 2007, long-passed 'historical revolution in orange' that took place barely three years ago.

There are only male breakfast guests. They shuffle their flip-flopped feet to the buffet, shovel fermented, pickled, sour and raw vegetables and meat onto their plates, displaying extreme skill in piling it as high as possible and carrying it back to their tables without spilling a single strand of grated white cabbage on the carpet.

They've all used the same shower gel to wash the sour smell off their well-trained bodies. In their tracksuits, they look as though they haven't yet decided whether to don a business suit with a shirt and tie before they leave the hotel afterwards, or rather camouflage fatigues.

The television is now showing a cadet comedy with subtitles – a Russian series, subtitled in Ukrainian for reasons of national sovereignty, or the other way around? Ten past nine. I haven't eaten yet. I'm smoking. Four aquariums, I count up here, and two more down in the foyer.

The flipflopped men pursue their morning matters – shovelling fermented food and gazing at military dress – quietly and routinely. No one pays attention to anyone else. I notice I'll soon run out of cigarettes, and I get nervous. I don't know anyone here who might give me a cigarette.

The world is set up anew every morning – what's the name of the world you arrive in in the morning? A breakfast room in

81

Kiev. Considered rationally, it corresponds pretty precisely with my idea of hell.

Not hot, not freezing cold, but just warm enough for everyone to want to wear German flipflops. Everyone but me. My fellow inmates haven't merely grown accustomed to the sour food, the smell of which wafts from the breakfast buffet every morning – in expectation of the expected, they've ordered it. Just as they wished to have the same shower gel provided in every shower. On television, the revolution continues every morning, only to intermingle with images from old TV shows every now and then. The offer of parading around as either a guerrilla fighter or a shrewd businessman for the rest of the day is also perfectly tailored to the wishes of this hell's inhabitants. And outside the window, an invisible hand pushes the sun – sentimentality rendered into light – into the sky, a sun you can tell comes, deliberately so, not from space but straight from a roll of photographic wallpaper.

*

Freudian slip as I read my own words back: 'The flipflopped men pursue their murder matters.'

*

The waste land. We've ended up by coincidence in this Palatinate village, with its merry-go-round in the market square, along with three rows of stalls – not a big deal, but here, where the next town is far away, apparently the event of the year. People have come together from the surrounding area, buying hot sausages and mushrooms, despite the August heat, as though they'd never eaten such exotic delights. After 10 minutes, we've seen everything and want to continue our journey, when we discover the bumper car ride on the margins. Though we're well beyond the age of simmering with excitement weeks ahead of the dodgems' arrival, the large luminous letters DISCO REGGAE SOUL TECHNO NEWS draw us magically.

The loud music, the announcer with his artificial intonation, the deliberate pile-ups on the polished floor, the screams and yells of the village teens – for anyone who grew up in the countryside, bumper cars have always embodied the big wide world. There were signs at the cash desk reading 'Young men wanted to travel', which made the boys aware they weren't old enough, despite their arrogant showmanship, and made the girls stare after the perhaps 20-year-old who pushed the cars to the sides when the music was over. The boys scraped their pocket money together for a few more plastic tokens while the girls got to ride for free, often enough: The 'young travelling man' stood proud on the back of the car with the village beauty queen in it and started her chariot with his master key, attached to a dangling foxtail.

None of that has changed to this day; the boys and girls still standing in separate groups, posing, giggling, casting worldly glances across the scenario, and it seems to me as if the songs they're playing are also the same as in the 1970s. There's an incredible energy in the air. I could hardly think of a greater contrast to the atmosphere T. S. Eliot conjures up in his poems: the poet imagined himself as an old man early on, and after the First World War sketched a tableau in *The Waste Land* with a darkness that undercoated the entire 20th century.

Now a group of girls overrun the bumper cars, all in strange bright-pink plush costumes, with paws and pricked ears and tails. They've probably just performed a jazz dance and can now let loose at last. I can't tell how old they are, but they aren't yet embarrassed by their outfits, happily wearing their painted-on whiskers and cat's noses in lieu of lipstick. They won't yet have heard of someone like T. S. Eliot, no laments of 'I grow old, I grow old,' for they have the wide world and adulthood ahead of them still.

But something about the pink cat suits won't let me go. I'd like to know why the girls have put on such shaggy monstrosities in this hot weather. They're driving their ceaseless circles, the first tipsy village lads turning up on the sidelines, the same Boney M song on the speakers as 10 minutes ago – when I realise: the girls must have performed a scene from *Cats*.

Cats, of course, everyone here knows it; the whole family might well have gone to the city to see *Cats*, which gave the girls the idea of learning a song and a few dance steps. And I can't help laughing, what with the lyrics to the musical being by none other than T. S. Eliot, a poet surely as unfamiliar with bumper cars as these village teens here are with his name.

*

The Joseph Beuys Travel Agency. At the station, a woman and her little daughter are ahead of me in the queue for the ticket booth. When the woman behind the glass asks for their destination, she murmurs something I don't understand, and the ticket seller too says, slightly amused but very friendly, 'Kiev? There aren't any trains to Kiev from Dresden.'

The customer murmurs again, more loudly: 'Kläv.'

And the ticket seller: 'Aha, Kleve.'

In Obervogelgesang, however, a small village upstream of us on the Elbe, the ticket machines on the platform, as we established with astonishment, can call up connections for the journey from Obervogelgesang to Moscow – provided you're clever enough to enter the spelling 'Moskwa' instead of 'Moscow' or indeed

'Moskau'. Departure 10:29, three changes, arrival at 17:54 the following day, total travel time 31 hours and 25 minutes.

V

There was nothing to see in my early poems. Perhaps that's why, when I try to remember them, one word comes to mind over and over, as though I were circling a blind spot in a vain attempt to get to its centre: Brixton. And with it a place, the neighbourhood in south London, and a certain weather, light, temperature, smells, glances. Everything lacking in my memory of the poems. Back then, I was a determined opponent of images, had an aversion to metaphors, wanted visible elements only in hazy form in my poems – there were no scenarios, specific spaces or places; no proper names which, no matter how unfamiliar, always point to something that can be registered by the eye.

I flick back and forth, getting annoyed, close to abandoning the attempt, losing myself along sidetracks. The first frayed pages will soon come loose from the spiral binding, and I have to admit, my *London A-Z* only helps me when I'm in London. I will have boarded a Victoria Line train either at Euston Square or Oxford Circus, both station announcements still equally clear in my ears. Whether I followed an instantaneous impulse, or my tube trip to south London was planned long before our group of a dozen sixth-formers ever reached the ferry to Dover, I no longer know. What I do know: on that October day in 1983, I was determined not to leave the train before the last stop. And I also remember one key, later frequent experience: you're the only white person here.

Driving into London by coach a few days previously, the whole English class had been amazed to spot the power station from the Pink Floyd record cover in the distance. I'd only ever heard Pink Floyd peripherally, when others listened to them. Now I was on my way to Brixton. It was a place I knew only by name, in written form, more clearly in songs. That was where I wanted to go. With a destination in mind, an address: 165 Railton Road. I was going to find the office of Race Today Publications.

Aside from me, only people I've never met personally are enthusiastic about things that fascinate me – that has always been something that goes without saying, no great disaster. Instead, I know the euphoria of discovering things for myself, and we rarely set out on journeys of discovery in large groups. During that week in London, I was magically attracted, in Chris Cutler's Recommended Records shop, to the gatefold cover of a single, Robert Wyatt's 'Shipbuilding' with details from a large painting of a shipyard. And 'Didn't Have A Very Good Time' by David Thomas, its title in retrospect as good a reflection of my mood at the time as 'Not Happy', the Pere Ubu single with which I left the Rough Trade label's shop the next day.

In Brixton, I stood around near the tube station for a while, undecided, intimidated. No chance of mingling inconspicuously with passers-by. Bargain stalls on the pavement, I remember shoes, crates of fruit and vegetables; I walked a little way and saw a bookshop on the corner, a haven for this bookish boy. I found three books by Linton Kwesi Johnson, the man whose publishing office I wanted to find here in the neighbourhood. Perhaps I got the address out of one of those slim volumes after all. Two poetry collections and a stage play: late offshoots of DIY-culture, largely hand-made A5 booklets, stapled, between 30 and 40 pages long with an ink drawing on the cover. Shortly before the trip to London, in August or September, I'd made my own poetry chapbook. And the appearance of Johnson's books may have granted me retroactive confirmation, for my poetry collection had looked like them.

I turned onto a long empty street. At the start of Railton Road there were a few shops and pubs, but the further I walked, the more entrances and windows were boarded up, whether because the houses were vacant, or becausethey'd been barricaded during the riots there two years previously. Inside number 165, I climbed the stairs, found a door marked 'RACE TODAY PUBLICATIONS' and knocked. After a while, several safety locks were unfastened from inside, a sound I knew only from TV. The door opened a crack.

A young white man in the hallway, not from round here. On second glance it's clear he's not police. His English isn't good. He doesn't even come from England. I don't know, did I introduce myself, did I tell them about my tours of the city, the books in my bag? I'd only envisaged the situation up to my asking whether Linton Kwesi Johnson was there. No. And the door was banged shut again. I went back out on the street and walked back through the authentic civil-war atmosphere to the tube. I wasn't disappointed.

Aside from me, only people I've never met personally are enthusiastic about things that fascinate me. Yet if I was now looking up addresses and roaming parts of London no tourist ever sets foot in, if I thought I might meet Chris Cutler in his record shop, Linton Kwesi Johnson in his publishing office, then my first poetry collection must have been a steppingstone:

I was stepping out of something, out of my condition perhaps, and thus also out of the poems collected in that chapbook. They were behind me, and when I recall them now, I find nothing in them, no echo of external events, the things that fascinated me. Were I not to possess the records from those days, the books from Brixton – my poems would give me no clue as to what moved me in 1983, what I perceived. Without this other writer's work, this music, that time would be deleted.

I shrug my shoulders at those poems now. What embarrassed me about the matter, shortly after I'd collected my book from the printers: our English teacher once said, visibly pleased, that he refused to respond to letters of complaint from parents who didn't know a space is needed after a comma. I'd never noticed that about commas and spaces. And so my first poetry collection was ruined for me by a comma comment, even before the trip to London.

The woman at the door – perhaps, it occurs to me now, the very first editor I ever saw – will have thought I was stupid. No, she'll have forgotten the disturbance right away. Linton Kwesi Johnson, someone who brought out books and records and saw himself confidently as a poet, not as a singer, for instance when he shared a stage with musicians – my two worlds overlapped in his person. And Chris Cutler, drummer, discoverer of obscure music, label-owner who hand-wrote his own distribution catalogues and the texts on the record covers of the Art Bears – Cutler, Dagmar Krause, Fred Frith – radiated the cool certainty, for me, that a person could both listen to music and read books. They both stood for an attitude that impressed me: they dedicated themselves to their cause without caring whether the so-called masses followed them, and that, funnily enough, coming from socialists. A minority programme without the slightest elitism, that's how I see it now, that's how I see my own work to this day.

Ten years later, in the summer of 1993, I was back in Brixton. The atmosphere in the neighbourhood had changed – a warm August evening, I'd arranged to meet Jah Shaka for an interview in the Supertone record shop at nine. By this point I regularly went to Supertone when I was in London. For an hour and a half, Jah Shaka spoke into my tape recorder in an assured, sonorous voice; he spoke of solidarity and Solidarność, of reggae's significance for the changes in Poland, spoke without the slightest sentimentality. Not even a touch of melancholia, as it slightly chokes me up standing outside the shipyard gates in Gdańsk today. At the end, he pressed a pile of singles upon me, white labels, printed only with the words: Jah Shaka Music.

I still listen to my singles from that October trip to London. I've only recently begun to discover Robert Wyatt's work. As though the music had laid a foundation back then, as though I'd been in a decisive phase. When it comes to my early poems, I wouldn't think of characterising them that way. Nor do I feel any impulse to reread them. There is nothing to see in them, after all.

In March 1986, I began working on *Das Menschenfleisch*; it was to become my fourth 'first' book. By then I hadn't been opposed to images for a long time, and yet it took me a while to let names, specific spaces, places, gazes appear in my writing. At 17 I'd soaked up London images, always kept them in mind – but they didn't find their way into my poems in those days. As though my brain was strictly divided between perception and writing. The abrupt end to that division is once again connected to a place: Vienna. In Vienna, which I visited increasingly frequently and for longer and longer stays from the mid-1980s, I found myself in a specific and magic place. I discovered the work of Friederike Mayröcker, I roamed Vienna's neighbourhoods, and suddenly every written sign I saw in the city, every word I picked up at a sausage stall had a place in a poem.

93

In 1989 I made *Kleine Zahnpasta* – A5, stapled – my second 'first' book, so as to have something to hold at readings while I waited impatiently for the publication of *Walkmännin*, the third. To this day, these pamphlets, swiftly Xeroxed affairs, have a special allure for me. One evening in the winter of 1996, shortly after the Docklands bombings, I found myself with artists in a pub on Railton Road. 1983 was long ago by then.

For me, it always went without saying: aside from me, only people I've never met personally are enthusiastic about things that fascinate me – perhaps this is where the unknown reader first comes into play. No disappointment, no desperation, more the formation of a perspective: there are people out there who are as enthusiastic as I am about a book, a record, and at the same time each of us lives in our own, occasionally dark world. It's not a matter or shared memories that impart a feeling of togetherness. Rather, we have memories of experiences each of us has had alone, perhaps had to have alone. Literature: a space I have to myself *and* share with others. When the poet Thomas Kling calls out a welcome in September 2004: 'Don Drummond rules OK!'... Or Ernst Jandl hands me a CD across the table in a Vienna pub garden in summer 1999, 'I thought this might interest you,' and it's a Fred Frith record...

*

Once again, I ask the curator of the Ornithological Collection to show us the contents of the drawers he'd prepared for the Museum Night two years ago, to give the lay visitors roaming from one exhibition hall to the next a rough insight into the ornithologist's work. No easy task, for the impression with which the visitors left the collection, otherwise open only to scholars, ought firstly to be sufficiently graphic that the imparted knowledge wouldn't be lost among the diffuse images that remain of such evenings of swiftly alternating experiences, and ought secondly to make no compromises at the expense of a scholar's precision and distinction, for instance in contrast to an amateur ornithologist. I remember it was a summer evening of heavy showers when we set off for the northern edge of Dresden, where the State Zoological Collection has been housed in a new building for some time now. We walked the corridors in excitement, stopping only briefly, so as to take in as much as possible, at each of the tables of preserved specimens with which the curators illustrated their specialist fields, only to then listen transfixed in the nest collection to a calm, emphatic voice debating ornithological issues between display cases and drawers, with all the care and candour of someone discussing the most ordinary wonders of the world.

The next day, perhaps that same night, I took notes that veritably flowed into lines, three stanzas, obvious even as I wrote them that they would become part of a longer poem with the title 'Earth Knowledge', which I was working on at the time:

> Once I saw pelts,
> lined up
> in their crate, goldfinches,
> varieties from all over
>
> the East. Some are around
> a hundred years old, no
> loss of colour, the head,
> the tail, the wings, and
>
> inside is padding. Only
> recently have their bones
> been also kept. I saw
> they lie well in the hand.

And now I'm back. Over the past two years, the first impression the goldfinch pelts made on me hasn't gradually faded to eventual nothingness, but rather taken on ever clearer contours as the occasion has grown more distant. Since that evening in summer 2001, I've been on the track of something, without noticing it at first. I watch the birds in the garden more attentively, consulting bird guides and enthusiastically studying newspaper articles on ornithological research – but I find it hard to believe that this entirely new interest should have been awoken solely by its object, these flying vertebrates we call birds. A mere object is not enough to captivate me to such an extent; there has to be some other thing. In this case, what triggered my movement towards ornithology must surely have been my observation of the way the object was handled: 'I saw they lie well in the hand.'

As he spread the items in his collection before us on our first encounter, the curator, Dr Siegfried Eck, pointed out how important the haptics of the individual avian skin are for a scholar's work, and now he repeats and demonstrates it, taking a crow collected in 1810 in his hand, feeling it carefully by cupping the feathers in his fingers, his lower arm bouncing gently as though to assess the pelt's weight, and he notes: This specimen comes from Father Brehm; he labelled and prepared it. Christian Ludwig Brehm, that extraordinary ornithologist and composer of a treatise on *The Art of Preparing Birds as Pelts*, was not actually very good at the task, the curator tells us; the bird is obviously stuffed with oakum, making it too hard and too heavy. A minor objection – the pelt is in excellent condition; Brehm Senior poisoned it with arsenic.

When I sensed that those three stanzas arising from the impression of a visit to the Ornithological Collection had not exhausted the image, the sight, but rather opened up a new world for me, I contacted the institution, which as I mentioned is only open to scholars, and asked the curator for a guided tour. He asked me why, and I hesitated at first to hint that it might be the beginning of a larger literary piece, but mere curiosity was not reason enough for him. I was a writer, I admitted, and two visual artists wanted to come to the collection with me – that sufficed. Looking back, I understand his openness to us laymen to mean he had no time for someone who merely wanted to gawp, but he saw an artist as a person who hopes to find something out by studying the objects with attentive patience. Not specialist visitors, then, but still someone whose approach to the object resembles that of a morphologist.

Sometimes, Dr Eck says, he sits for weeks before a number of pelts spread out on his desk, attempting to sort them. Forty to fifty stuffed individuals, hitherto seen as belonging to the same species – a view in which he has doubts, without being able to substantiate those doubts, let alone prove the opposite. It is a suspicion at first, perhaps only an inkling that the birds in fact belong to at least two species, albeit very closely related, of course. There are no vocal profiles or genetic analyses in this case, so he forms ever new groups; lays out the birds in front of him in order of inconspicuous characteristics; pushes one pelt hesitantly back and forth between one row and another, this hesitation leading him to conclude that the existing order cannot be correct; begins anew with different criteria, his concentrated study profoundly familiarising him with the details of every single pelt; memorises each individual's beak and feathering; breathes the specific scent of these birds from morning to night, yet does not come to a satisfactory conclusion. Then at some point, after weeks of doubting and waiting and studying, it happens, everything goes very quickly: on a recent occasion, he managed by this method to prove, on the basis of the outer appearance of certain pelts, that they weren't one, as previously assumed, but three different species.

He can imagine, he says, that an artist's work might occasionally be rather similar. A sudden recognition: That's how it must be, that's how the elements are related. And the immediate question: Why didn't I see it straight away? I answer in my mind: Because the sorting, the often-torturous waiting and the nonetheless continuing, precise observation are a necessary part of the work. It is a practice in dealing with respective objects, be it avian skins, colours or language.

And so, as the curator pulls out the drawer of goldfinch pelts and puts it on the table, I experience a curious situation: an ornithologist, about whose work I've written a short poem without his knowledge, explains to me, on the basis of his work, how writing might take place. Or to be precise: by cautiously formulating possible analogies between artistic and ornithological work, he attempts to illustrate the procedures of an ornithologist specialised in exploring the exterior form of birds.

The analogies seem so plausible, the representation of his way of working so familiar, that I permit myself to report on these two visits to the Ornithological Collection in this contemplation on writing poetry. I could nod non-stop as I listen to Dr Eck and translate his comments to the business of poetry: for example, when it comes to patterns of describing evolution, the question of adaptation. Old-fashioned picture-book thinking is widespread, he tells us: Why are a chicken's legs as long as they are? So that they reach the ground. That gives us a nice explanation, but that explanation is utter nonsense. It sounds, it occurs to me, suspiciously like a common procedure in German lessons.

What he's interested in, he says, is proximities; his primary goal is to recognise and describe differences. That's exactly what poems are, I think, not postulates of any kind of wisdom that prove at first glance to be gubbins, but explorations of proximities; not diffuse expressions of inner feelings, but words placed

98

in relation to one another with the greatest possible clarity. In both cases, it's a matter of kinship, not fraternisation. That too shows that poems and, for example, current New Age phenomena are incompatible. Those who understand self-help literature to mean self-affirmation ought to stay away from poetry. Those who shudder at the thought of primal screams, the harmony of the spheres, recitations with gong accompaniment, and the inner child might think of becoming an ornithologist or reading poetry. Poems are research – in a different field to natural sciences, by different means and with a different subject, of course, but similar in their motions. With one distinct divergence: In poems, a research motion can be traced, but poems are not aimed at research outcomes, unlike the work of an ornithologist, for example. Poems have no outcome.

The proximities, the differences, the gaze: even the two still common German names for the same bird offer material and marvel enough: the etymologically unclear Slavic *Stieglitz* and the immediately illustrative *Distelfink*, thistle finch. Not long after coming across the goldfinch pelts, I discover the same bird species in Thomas Kling's *Sondagen*, also in 12 lines, which are again part of a larger piece. Perhaps, I think with excitement, we both worked on a thistle finch/goldfinch poem at the same time, each with his own finch in mind, unaware of one another as we wrote:

this head-
patch, headpatch;

(finks: thistles)

mark on the crown like
arterial blood.

standing out,
from frost; swing-
ing from dangling blade
the red (thistlefink): what

a beautiful pair
of thistle finches.

*

How long is the path from *shchegól* to *chardonneret*?

How many languages find space on one bird?

On my first visit to Leuk in Valais, I heard it said that on certain
days of the year with particularly favourable weather, you can,
looking down into the Rhône Valley, make out the river's delta
on the horizon, and even the sea. I ought to have been suspicious,
but before I knew better, and without a map in sight, I initially
took the words as mere information – perhaps possible distrust
was also overpowered by an inner voice: What do *you* know, a
man who understands only fragments of the Valais dialect and
as good as no French, of the things that occur before your eyes
beyond the language boundary; how could you judge whether
the matter of the distant sea view is true when you're not even

capable of recognising the nearby spot where the Rotten, fed by the Rhône glacier, finally flows into the Rhône?

Language boundaries, there is no doubt, can also be perceived optically, more easily in some places because additional changes accompany the language shift, the course of a political or geographical border, for instance, or because the transition from one language to another is fluid. But even where border lines and landscape shifts are lacking, I am convinced the linguistic boundary will be visible, provided we contemplate it with patience and a focused eye.

But does the existence of a language boundary also affect those who cross it? Do I change recognisably when I set out for Sitten only to arrive in the end in Sion, every time?

The promise of seeing the Mediterranean from the surrounding mountains reminded me of a story. Some 130 years ago, a 15-year-old boy from Ukraine, a boy later to call himself Joseph Conrad, underwent a westward journey with his Polish tutor, via Vienna, the upper Danube, Munich and Lake Constance into Switzerland. A journey with the goal of gently dissuading the boy from his desired profession. The inland waterways, the broad land, the large cities, finally the Alps: against the backdrop of this widening of horizons, the dream of going to sea would soon pale, hoped his guardian and the teacher accompanying him. 'It was an excellently appropriate arrangement, as neither he nor I had ever had a single glimpse of the sea in our lives,' Joseph Conrad would later write.

The plan made far away in Ukraine didn't succeed. 'Of late we had been tramping slowly up the valley of the Reuss.' – 'Landing from a Lake of Lucerne steamer in Fluellen, we found ourselves at the end of the second day, with the dusk overtaking our leisurely footsteps, a little way beyond Hospenthal.' – 'Our mapped-out route led over the Furca Pass towards the Rhône

Glacier, with the further intention of following down the trend of the Häsli Valley.' ('Häsli Valley' rather than the correct name, Hasli Valley. I love this kind of error – as though some third party, the typesetter perhaps, or in my case the translator into German, had adopted a child's perspective, a child Conrad has not been for some time by the point of this journey, and added umlauts to change the valley into one inhabited by bunnies, or *Häschen* in High German.) The two young men were thus on their way to the Valais, the teacher talking to his pupil incessantly along the way to persuade him against going to sea, presumably speaking Polish in the foreign language surroundings, perhaps French, and then something occurred 'in full view of the Finster-Aarhorn, with his band of giant brothers rearing their monstrous heads against a brilliant sky,' as Conrad writes; something that made the tutor cave in, abandon his intent: on the Furca Pass, the two of them came across an English-speaker. English, right there in the Alps: the language of the greatest seafaring nation. A few English words and the Polish-speaking tutor gives in. A year later, his pupil signs up on board his first ship in Marseille.

Neither he nor his teacher had ever seen the sea at that point, Conrad writes, yet once the life-changing decision has been made, we learn nothing more of their descent to the Rhône Valley. Not a word on whether teacher and pupil crossed another language border, here from the foreign Swiss-German side back into familiar French. Who knows, perhaps the two of them, approaching Leuk, got to savour the aforementioned weather conditions, and perhaps they made out the sea on the horizon.

Do I change recognisably when I cross a language boundary?

How long is the path from *shchegól* to *chardonneret*?

Reading an excellent book on the fauna of Valais, I flick to the back and look up goldfinch in the index, but the *Stieglitz* doesn't appear. *Steinschmätzer, Stelze, Stockente, Storch* – might the goldfinch, I wonder for a fraction of a second, not inhabit Valais? Of course it does; I search the index for the Latin name and find it immediately: *Carduelis carduelis*, the thistle finch; its second name of *Stieglitz* is clearly not used in Valais. Or the fauna guide defines its 'index of German-Latin species names' very precisely; *Stieglitz* comes from the Slavic, the syllable '-itz' clearly indicating its origins.

Where, though, at what point when we imagine this bird's journey, looking from the east towards Valais, does it change its name; where does the *Stieglitz* appear and where is it lost?

In Russian: *shchegól*, in Polish: *szczygiel*, in Czech: *stehlík*, then, switching into eastern German, essentially still Slavic regions: *Stachlick, Stechlitz, Stichlitz, Stiegelitzsch, Sterlitze* and *Stieglitz*. Linguistically mixed zones, where names – now largely forgotten – like *Kletter, Goldfink, Fistelfink, Distel-Zeisig, Distelvogel* and finally *Distelfink* join them.

Shchegól – szczygiel – stehlík – Stachlick – Stieglitz – Distelfink. That might have been the approximate route by which a Russian *Carduelis carduelis* had pursued the young Konrad Korzeniowski to Valais. Following the linguistic route, the rather hapless explanation that the *Stieglitz* got its name due to its call of 'stigelit' appears nothing but nonsense thought up by lazy language learners: we ought to listen less to the bird's call than to what it is called in Slavic languages.

But is there space on this bird, in Valais, for only a single name aside from its Latin designation? No, it occurs to me; just like in eastern Saxony, here I am in a linguistic border region, and my guide to the fauna of Valais is translated from French. And if I look it up in my French-German dictionary, I find the same word under *Distelfink* as under *Stieglitz: chardonneret*.

Perhaps then there is only ever room on a bird for two names at any one time and in any one place, besides the Latin, and thus in Valais, where the French *chardonneret* joins the German *Distelfink*, the long-carried Slavic-rooted *Stieglitz* must fall aside.

'The power of sound', Joseph Conrad once wrote, 'has always been greater than the power of sense.' The path from the Russian *shchegól* to *Distelfink* is a long one. Yet if I take a few steps to the southwest from this point, the *Distelfink* becomes the *chardonneret*, and suddenly it seems as though I'd been moving, in terms of sound, almost in a circle. *Stieglitz* and *Distelfink* disappear, and all that remains is the adjacency of *chardonneret* and *shchegól*.

One passage in Pierre-Alain Oggier's fauna book captivates me in particular – perhaps because there is an inkling here that birdwatching differs from trainspotting, for instance because the question of the relationship between word and object is always invoked. The passage reads: 'Numerous winter guests arriving from the cold are not even noticed among the native birds. How could we tell a chaffinch from the forests of Sweden from its Valais cousins, or a robin from the Taiga from one from the Alps?'

The question is asked rhetorically, as if decided – for me, however, it sounds more like a question to which there is no answer. Of course, the robin from the Taiga goes through no visible changes by crossing the language boundary. But it does become a different robin. If only for someone writing about it.

The *bofink* from Sweden, then the *malinovka*, a feminine creature from Russia: she who lives in the raspberry bush: for us Germans, our red-throated *Rotkehlchen*. And, to go with it, the Russian *ryabinnik*: he who lives in the rowan tree: the fieldfare, in German *Wacholderdrossel* or juniper thrush, initially a winter guest in the 1950s, now seen breeding in Valais and thus a new native.

How can we differentiate them from the native birds? – By their names, linguistically, between the languages.

As for Joseph Conrad, who heard his first words of English in Valais, later began to write, and one day returned to Switzerland to work on his first novel in Geneva, whereby 'the sun of my sea-going was setting, too, even as I wrote the words' – for the Polish- and French-speaking Conrad there was only one alternative: either writing in English or not writing at all.

*

A translator takes a walk above Lake Geneva, and psyche lights upon the words. 'I don't believe in bilingualism in poetry,' Paul Celan once replied with determination to an enquiry. Might there, however, be a multilingualism of plants and animals, as they move from place to place, from one time to another?

Psyche: the butterfly, *Sommervogel, Molkendieb, Schmetterling* – summer bird, whey thief, cream thing.

'It was better yesterday, especially after I had called you from Nyon,' Paul Celan writes in a touching letter to his wife, a long Sunday letter that touches on much, about a day trip on 29 September 1962, on Celan's rather interminable first weekend in Geneva, where he had arrived a few days previously to work as a translator at the International Labour Office.

From Nyon, he reports, he had taken a small train up to Saint-Cergue; sunny weather, very few people, forests all around, and: 'all trees – very mixed, from the rowan to the larch – still had their leaves – you would have liked to walk here: I thought of that.' There, he had taken his afternoon coffee on a hotel terrace, 'in the company of words for a poem, scribbled down in Nyon.'

Forty-four years later, in early September 2006, I take the same day trip, tracing the route of Paul Celan's walk. On the winding narrow road to Saint-Cergue, through the fields, I was welcomed by butterflies, a bird of prey circling in the sky, a lizard on the sun-warmed tarmac of a curve in the road. Up in the village, I find an old, long-closed restaurant for day-trippers opposite the station; perhaps Celan sat here over his poem notes. On the glazed terrace are two empty aviaries and, as the grimy awnings reveal, the place was most recently called 'Chez Charly'.

'Then I decided,' Celan writes to his wife, 'to walk down to Arzier, via a short-cut given to me by the landlady. It was beautiful, very beautiful, walking up there, and all at once, I was not at all prepared for it, a flower appeared on my right: a *Zeitlose* – a flower called 'timeless'. Here, the reader pauses. Like his geological German, Paul Celan's botanic German makes him stand proud of our contemporary poetry, so clear and resistant that some knew no better than to think it an invention of a second-language-speaker from Romania. Yet here, with the flower name 'Zeitlose', the autumn crocus, or *Herbstzeitlose*, it becomes clear once again – the Celans corresponded in French, and Eugen Helmlé translated their letters into German. How does Celan, on this slow-moving Sunday, show this inherently timeless flower to his wife? He writes 'colchique', and thus he switches, despite appearing to remain in French, into another language. More than that: he switches language, time and place. That's how he goes into the poem.

He asks: 'Do you remember the poem before last: "Columbus, die Zeitlose im Aug, die Mutterblume"? – And there I thought of the very last poem, written after the letter received from Moscow, in which Erich Einhorn told me he would be spending his holidays in "Kolchis", that is, on the Black Sea.' *Colchicum autumnale*: the autumn crocus. Colchis: Ovid's exile, Mandelstam land.

106

There is no landlady these days to ask for a shortcut; instead, just beyond the road and parallel to the railway line, a newly sign-posted hiking trail into the forest, along the Jura slopes, which I follow – rather hastily, as I will later realise. The rugged abyss to my right, and on the left, between the trees, repeated glimpses of soft, warm-tinted chalk cliffs, I walk towards the valley.

"'Kolchis,'" Celan writes, 'that was, and I only realised this yesterday, only a secret echo of the "Zeitlose", evoked by reality.' On the sight of a flower and the question of its name, he sees himself far away in the east, transported to the Black Sea; sees Erich Einhorn nearby, his childhood friend; sees himself simultaneously in ancient Roman times and with Ossip Mandelstam. And, as he translates the sight of a flower, he is borne into a poem of his own, 'And with the Book from Tarussa':

> Of the adverb, which
> a rower crunches, into the late-summer lugs
> of his keen-
> eared thowel:
>
> colchis.

Butterflies here, too. Where the trail turns slightly to the north, a spot has been cleared, a viewing place created. Down by the lake, covered by a light layer of vapour as if beneath glass, and above the snow-topped peaks of the four-thousanders in the blue-white sky, a moon soon to be full. If I try hard, I think I can make out Montreux in the distance.

I wonder whether Celan looked out over Lac Léman from this spot like me, and whether he knew at the time that Vladimir Nabokov had settled on the opposite shore the previous year, crossing languages and collecting butterflies since his Russian childhood.

Then I look down upon Nyon, the small town at the foot of the Jura, not finding any fortifications in the townscape, no tower before the backdrop of the lake, nor the castle 'with which you will, I am sure, be familiar,' as Rainer Maria Rilke writes – in the foreword to the picture story by 11-year-old Balthus, which begins with views of Nyon Castle, and a tom-cat named Mitsou.

Later, Rilke writes about the 'Slavic temperament' of his 'little friend', and: 'he originates from an old Polish family, Klossowski, one branch of which, however, had become German for two generations, in Silesia; not very thoroughly.'

Der Schmetterling, the butterfly: witches, they say, appear in the form of butterflies to rob farmers of milk and cream, unrecognised. I'm not certain whether this interpretation captures a folk belief or a folk etymology, but I don't doubt the explanation that *Schmetterling* is a word that comes from far away in the East: *Schmetter*, in Silesian, is cream, and *Schmetterling* half-borrowed from the Slavic surroundings – *smetana*: Czech for cream.

Celan continues: 'A little further – the fields were soon strewn with autumn crocuses – as I left the road to take the path to the goat-shed, there was another flower: eyebright – *Augentrost – l'euphraise –* about which I have told you rather often, I believe. In the war, in Moldova, loaded down with two pails (water? soup?) that I was to fetch to the small town before noon, to take them to the "building site", I had come across this *Augen-Trost.'*

Eyebright. The labour-camp flower, *Augentrost*, meaning solace for the eye, now in both German and French, side by side, 'l'euphraise', close to the Latin *Euphrasia officinalis –* 'there, you see, I saw myself cast back,' he writes, and he goes on walking. On the path, he spots silver thistles and rowans, spots words: with the rowan leaves in mind, he realises how he has to translate a line from Yesenin – the sight of a bush in French, to take him from Russian to German. When he faces the choice of beating a path through the forest or turning back, his courage abandons him, and he turns back.

A long weekend alone, during which Paul Celan encounters the autumn crocus. Down in Nyon, on rue Perdtemps, the genuinely existing time-wasting street not far from the castle, he made these notes for a poem, among other things:

> Come via Kraków, on the
> November train. At Anhalter Station
> the smoke floated toward your gaze.
> That was to be – what was to be?
> discussed, from elsewhere.

He enclosed an autumn crocus with his letter, and three weeks later he was to take the same day trip again, accompanied by his wife. She knows what the German-language flower, what 'Augentrost' means to him. Up to that point, the word appears only once in his poems, in September 1942, and it is suspected the poem may have been written on the day that Celan, in the labour camp, heard of his deported father's death.

To me, however, it soon becomes clear that I haven't been following in Paul Celan's footsteps at all, here on the wolf's path that crosses no fields. Now I beat a path through the forest, back up, across the railway line towards the sound of cattle bells. There, a clearing, a meadow – the farmer has just milked his cows, lit a small fire; he is cleaning utensils, and switches off the generator for the milking machine. At some point I reach a road, the road to Saint-Cergue, and a sign shows me I've been walking the path to the goats' stall in the opposite direction.

I haven't seen autumn crocuses or eyebrights. Certainly – like words and images, flora and fauna are unique and appear only to each individual, phenomena which resist generalisation. There is no such thing as shared fate, just like poems cannot be shared. And, above Lake Geneva, I cannot repeat Paul Celan's flower-spotting, nor his path through the languages. That is a skill possessed perhaps only by the butterfly.

Yet we could linger, at the sight of a butterfly, in the space between languages – a gentle breath, and we feel pain and euphoria at our proximity to the faraway places and the dead, be it only for a wingbeat:

> If it will soothe my terror of the void
> To characterise butterflies as souls
> And summer visions of the vanished dead.

Thus, psyche flutters through the languages in Inger Christensen's 'Butterfly Valley', as translated by Susanna Nied; flutters from Danish via Greek into English, and to me, via Norbert Hummelt's German version, back into its Slavic landscape. Thus, psyche lights upon the words.

'A secret echo, evoked by reality,' as Paul Celan writes, and: 'One ought to know how to be satisfied with this kind of dialogue – a little extra-human, don't you think?'

VI

On the book cover, we see the writer at work: She is standing behind an open multi-storey hive, sweeping bees from a well-filled Zander frame, back into the honey super, with a soft bee brush. Bees are crawling around on the frame, several brown spots in the air in the background, but most appear to have withdrawn deep into the body still holding full combs, the smoker having been used a few moments previously. The beekeeper is wearing a short-sleeved blouse, no gloves, no hat. A picture of extreme concentration. An image of reflection. Extreme command of the body. Command of language.

A lucky find. *Mein Bienenjahr – My Bee Year. A Working Calendar for the Apiarist* by Lieselotte Gettert – I was guided solely by the title when choosing the book, the interplay of poetry and practicality exerting a magical attraction. A testimonial of 40 years of beekeeping, designed as an introduction for beginners, and an insight into her own work for colleagues, far removed from keeping any secrets. A call for dialogue, bee considerations, in 12 clearly constructed chapters from January through to December; this *Working Calendar* is exactly what it promises. The main title, meanwhile, promises something else, the possessive pronoun and the suggestive expression *Bee Year* opening up a broad field that we, the readers, writers, move through like honey-making insects, in the book, on our honeybee meadow. We don't keep bees, we don't make honey, we collect neither honeydew nor pollen – and that's why *Mein Bienenjahr* reads as a work that could scarcely be imagined in more concise form, telling us something about writing and also showing us how writing can be done.

'Absolute peace now prevails among the bees.' A simple sentence, a clear observation which the lay reader can understand with no effort, formulated in a confident, relaxed tone that will guide us through the 12 chapters of this 'working calendar'. 'Absolute peace now prevails among the bees.' What a magnificent opening to a bee book, in January, 'in the apiary' – there is nothing for us, the observer, the beekeeper, to see, nothing to do.

To feel the momentum of that first sentence, a reader has to get all the way to the end of the December chapter, as I realise now that I've flicked back to the beginning, and perhaps we ought also to recall the opening passages of other bee books; images of spring, bee meadows, hymns to honey, or solemn instructions for present-day beekeeping inferred from the long history of human–honeybee coexistence. By contrast, Lieselotte Gettert, is casual and precise: in January, anyone who dares approach a beehive will see that nothing is happening.

The reader is instantly spellbound. This beekeeper knows how to build such tension in a sentence of seven simple words that we sense it will inevitably be released in the following lines. That is how classic winter images work: the white surface, scant light, no motion. Then, an invasion of nature's force, or the appearance of a human who will bring everything toppling down. She who shows us January's empty canvas will no doubt soon sketch in the first traces of the coming catastrophe. *Doctor Zhivago* thrives upon it, *James Bond* regularly demonstrates it on the screen, and with its white pages, *Tintin in Tibet* consistently evokes all the reader's expectations of snowy images.

Gettert expands the arsenal of emptiness by adding a new variant, in which she drafts with swift strokes two tragedies in the subjunctive mood: firstly, even 'the tremor on entering an apiary or handling a hive stand' can mean a life-threatening disruption for the hibernating bees; 'the colony surges, temperature and feed levels rise' – the topos of disaster-bringing man. Secondly, the fatal force of nature, here in the form of snow, which gathers outside the entrances if there's been a heavy fall: 'The snow may be air-permeable, but when it thaws and then freezes again, the bees may be in danger.' In either case, *My Bee Year* would be over within barely a quarter of a page, any narrative now possible only in retrospect.

A simple observation of nothing is followed by the author's concentrated knowledge; the guileless layman's view meeting the beekeeper's endless imagination. It has taken no more than two brief dramatic paragraphs – the beekeeper could hardly have found a better way to draw us into her world of bees. Only now do we grasp what we accepted in that opening scene, without complaining, as we usually do, about all this terminology that we lay readers don't understand. On the contrary, guided by the beekeeper's confident voice, full of expectations, we have gained a vague image of a 'hive stand', of the 'feed level' and of 'surging', and though we sense we cannot clearly define the meaning of these words, we can, trusting in the beekeeper, leave them in the text as unfamiliar material, as foreign interjections, as little patches of white, without anticipating disaster.

Perhaps we also sense at this point that it would do us no good to interrupt the flow, to withdraw from the author's gaze

115

and flick to the end of the book – behind her back, as it were – to look things up in the index and then, as though nothing had happened, return to the beginning as clever beekeeping students – though of course, you would scour the index in vain for entries like 'surge', 'hive stand' or 'feed level'. And does Gettert not use, in her very second sentence, a 'we'; an open invitation to stay close because she intends to grant us insights into the beehive?

Making observations and finding words for them. Acquiring vocabulary and using it on the things we see. These two motions interlock so closely that they cannot be separated. Those of us with no experience of beekeeping are constantly coming across terms, the meanings of which only become clear to us through other terms. We encounter dark spots in the text which even the numerous photographic illustrations cannot illuminate – a particular speciality, it seems to me, of bee books. Thus, having thought I had an approximate understanding of the term 'foundation', on seeking a definition I had to concede that I could neither explain what 'foundation' means exactly, nor what foundation is used for. Why is it placed where into a hive body, and when? I'm certain the meaning would be immediately clear to me if I were to watch a beekeeper at work, without a word of explanation.

We have thus learned a first lesson at the very beginning of January, while absolute peace prevails among the bees: we ought not to get aggravated when we come across unfamiliar words, as it only burns energy unnecessarily – which can be fatal in winter. Better to concentrate on the text. Should we weaken, let us reach for the honey jar. Unfamiliar vocabulary: unexpected peeps through the entrance, into another world, in there, out here. Either we follow the beekeeper's voice patiently month by month through the year, or we perish immediately as our entrances freeze over.

What does that mean, though: month by month through the bee year? In her second January section, Lieselotte Gettert has us consider: 'I would not like to say the bee year begins at this or that point.' Let us take the openings of two famous bee books to support her, *The Adventures of Maya the Bee* by Waldemar Bonsels, 1912, and *The Dancing Bees* by Karl von Frisch, 1927. 'The elderly lady-bee who helped the baby-bee Maya when she awoke to life and slipped from her cell was called Cassandra and commanded great respect in the hive,' Bonsels begins, and: 'Those were exciting days. A rebellion had broken out in the nation of bees, which the queen was unable to suppress.' Swarming season, in other words; the hive over-populated after a long hatching period, and the queen would also appear to have pheromonal problems. The date: mid-May.

Karl von Frisch gives us a broader context, in his introductory sentences, of how man and bee might meet: 'There are two ways by which the amateur naturalist may easily get acquainted with honey-bees. He can either walk through an orchard or a field full of flowers on a warm spring or summer's day and watch the bees busy foraging at the blossoms; or, passing a bee-keeper's apiary, he may see them flying in and out of the entrances of their hives.' Setting the first pollen collection as the earliest date, the bee year thus begins – depending on the weather – at some point in March. January is mentioned nowhere.

Yet because Gettert has undertaken to write a *Working Calendar for the Apiarist*, human time and bee time clash by necessity from the very beginning. 'The life of bees,' she writes, 'like all life, is a constant cycle.' Determining a starting point can only ever be done with caveats: 'Many set this beginning in July, when the colony prepares for winter. But then our house colonies must have developed well for some time, and honey colonies should still have spruce flow.' Even the detailed question of when exactly the bee year begins makes it clear we are dealing with highly complex yet fragile structures we can never fully understand. And depending on our perspective, it seems as though the construction itself may change as our idea of it changes. 'Absolute peace now prevails among the bees.' What if that opening sentence does not mark the beginning of the year at all, nor the beginning of the book?

By going into the incompatibility of the human and bee calendars in her first chapter, Gettert indirectly points us to another quality of her *Working Calendar*. As with every stimulating book, *My Bee Year* contains, alongside the immediately recognisable structure, a pattern of partially concealed structures, occasionally hinted at by the author through cross-references but also possible for us to discover for ourselves, following our own clues. To begin with, we will be guided by the narrative, making observations of the apiary month by month; in a second stage, we will glean general bee knowledge from these observations, and then follow the necessary work steps. Soon, however, repeated motifs come to the fore, and we are drawn back to earlier passages because we missed an important detail which is now required to proceed – thus, we are already working on our own text.

In February, for instance, positive experiences with tansy as smoking material are mentioned. In July we see its yellow umbels in a colour photograph. At the end of August, we will at last gather tansy, chop it and dry it on large tarpaulins. Smoking material for February – in the book, however, February has long since passed.

Every lay reader knows an aggressive bee can be recognised by its particular flight sound. Reading *My Bee Year*, I noted at several points the role of sounds in the balance between beekeeper and honeybee. 'If concerned as to whether a colony is still alive, listen closely at an entrance,' the author recommends for the wintertime, when there is nothing to see: 'you will hear a gentle hum and know everything is fine.' In the opposite direction, the bee perceives what is going on outside the dark hive and determines physical presence on the basis of sounds. Thus, the beekeeper must ensure that no windswept branches scratch against the hive in winter; otherwise the bees become agitated, dysentery breaks out, and the colony dies. Acoustics and temperatures, the wellbeing of the bees and their keeper: Perhaps, were I to read more closely with this aspect in mind, an almost invisible web might be spun throughout the book.

Many things occur unseen, in beekeeping. For instance, on the occasion of the first spring check in April, when we inspect a double colony, that is, a colony living in two vertically stacked bodies: 'We do not yet check the bottom, provided the colony seems calm.' We can draw conclusions from the goings-on in the upper body for the goings-on in the bottom section. 'The lower space, where most of the field bees are and which is mainly used for occasional pollen storage, remains untouched by us all summer.' Beekeeping has to do with discretion.

We read the bees, and as we do so we wonder: How are the bees reading me? The apiary is a site of continuous coding and decoding. An illustration of this principle, obligatory in every bee book: those who are afraid get stung. The sweat triggered by fear makes bees aggressive.

The beekeeper bent over the open hive, her gaze turned away from the observer, focused on the narrow space between the honeycomb and the bee brush, her entirety an expression of fearless concentration. The bees know their mistress, we might think, she can approach them unprotected, for neither will harm the other. 'I prefer to work without a veil, with a light coat or sleeveless in the heat of summer,' she writes, and: 'We don't wear gloves; they hinder our work.'

How, then, does she protect herself from stings? She has to exude invincibility towards the bees. Calm, swift, focused movements are very important, naturally. More important yet is scent. Never signal fear through sweat on the skin – you might say a good beekeeper knows how to latch directly onto her colonies' pheromones. Gloves or a protective suit would imbalance this calming exchange of scents. Aside from which, glovelessness not only enables fast, precise work; the bare hand also acts as a signal to the beekeeper herself, regulating her own pheromone release in turn. A form of self-assurance: I see I can put my bare hand into my colonies, I feel no fear, and thus I am invulnerable to possible attacks. Here, the beekeepers' gradually attained immunity to beestings comes into play, their bodies refusing to regard the sting as an attack to be met with an allergic reaction or a counterattack. I know no enemies – and that makes me invulnerable.

And not least, Lieselotte Gettert's extensive experience of touching bees also contributes to her invulnerability. In the June chapter, she gives a brief, impressive report on how she – the child of a beekeeping household – was tasked during her training to mark virgin queens with an adhesive dot: 'It was important to hold the bees by the thorax in such a way as not to get stung (bees only move their abdomens upwards and downwards, not from side to side). Not until a number of worker bees had survived the procedure was I allowed to mark queens.' Practice on individual insects, with bare fingers, as an acquisition of tactile bee knowledge.

Touch and scent, attention to velocity and, of course, colours: the beekeeper has thought her way into these insects' world through repeated, precise dealings with them, built herself a set of antennae. The author appreciates her bees because she knows very well how to evaluate them. Yet I am certain another trait is of perhaps decisive importance for the success

120

of her work, and I think we can read it in the photo of the honey harvest, in the gaze Gettert casts upon the swept frame: she may have gathered never-ending bee knowledge – yet she shows how well she knows that these creatures will never lose their mystery.

That enquiring eye upon the honey chamber: an exercise in controlled wandering. Every hand movement at the apiary is rehearsed, follows a minutely choreographed plan only altered when the unexpected happens or is observed, in the colony, in the hive, on the combs. An amateurish flinch, indeed even an unprofessional, curiosity-driven morning check would bring agitation to the colony and lead to a loss of honey production.

For a beekeeper, there is no 'natural' movement above the open Zander frame, just as there is no such thing as natural speech. Everything is staged, artificial, following rules or indeed diverging from a set of rules. Let us send to an apiary those who think that language is simply there, a given, and that writing means merely chatting on paper. There are no natural sentences.

Nature? Treetrunk hive, Lüneburg skep, Kanitz basket, Dathe twin hive, German standard hive, Slovenian AZ hive, Nenniger-Hoehn three-frame 'Universal' hive, Golz horizontal top-bar hive, Bremer top-bar hive, Langstroth hive, Dadant hive, Segeberg plastic hive, the Hofmann hive, also referred to as the Alpentrog hive, Zander hive, a.k.a. Zander standard-sized multiple-storey hive, Erlangen multiple-storey hive and Hohenheim hive. This short list alone of artificial homes for bees makes it obvious how close the relationship between human and honeybee is. Breeding-bees, which can prove unpredictable. The beekeeper knows of the intensity of her interventions in bee society. In the hive, nature and culture meet in the closest of quarters. Thus, the language in *My Bee Year* testifies to a high level of reflection – only in this way can it deliver a clear picture of the observed processes. And it's up to us to study that beekeeper's perspective.

The highly coded dealings with bees find expression in the language. Would we choose to place our frames the cold or the warm way? Of course, the warm placement may be less practical, but a writer can hardly resist the prospect of flicking through an AZ hive. The inexhaustible beekeeper's dictionary. Mental precision and plasticity hand in hand. Those not observing with full presence of mind automatically reveal themselves to be mentally lazy. And precision of observation yields mysterious words. Here, we see: the poetic is the precise.

Little by little, we acquire this vocabulary in *My Bee Year*, following descriptions that seem familiar in part, introduced as new, necessary movements in a respective month and thus bringing us into contact with words unknown. That is far better than combing through a glossary of apiculture, for instance – the alphabetical order fails to reveal how the individual steps interlock, how and where human and bee meet, or how the words interact. The meaning of a word is its use at the apiary.

Practical, clear – and yet of shimmering darkness. At times, shuffling the elements within a composite suffices to open up a previously unknown world. No one will confuse a tree hive with a hive tree – the latter is a natural bee home, the former used to be man-made, based on nature. The colony is 'an entire organism consisting of many individual creatures, none of which is capable of survival alone, only all members together with combs and housing (the hive),' as Lieselotte Gettert explains to us.

Words that – but it cannot be this way – seem to change their meaning depending on the context. Words for which I try to guess the meaning along aural recollections. Nurse colony, breeder colony, honey colony, house colony. I learn to separate the brood chamber from the honey chamber. But how exactly does the escape chamber differ from the drum chamber? Does the words' meaning start buzzing here? Are there, contrary to expectations, synonyms in beekeeping language, though its poetic rigour seems to me to be immune to the misunderstanding that terms can be interchangeable? Prime swarm and after-swarm. Virgin queen swarm and hunger swarm. Natural swarm and artificial swarm. A swarm is 'taken', a super 'put on'. If the 'drone battle' does not take place in August and no dead males are found around the entrance, Gettert takes this as a sign that a colony 'still wants a supersedure' – a process 'over which the colony must decide; the beekeeper should not intervene.'

I, however, am unsettled by this queen supersedure. I see myself seeking a queen cup for signs of queenrightness. Language acquisition is almost automatically stimulated when dealing with bees. Work is going well at the solar wax extractor. I watch a colony being taken in a skep, where plenty of fanning is going on, of course. As a reader, I make involuntary bibliographies of unwritten books, *Swarm Prevention*, *The Bee-Breeder's Basket*, *Recollections from the Honey House*, *Queen-Mating Stations Then and Now*, *Brood of Laying Workers* or *Experiences with Carniolan Drone-Laying Queens* – I want to read every one of them. And there goes my cappings scratcher along the bottom board. Magic. Pheromones. Reading beekeeping language immediately prompts verbal comb-building.

Is it beekeeping's vicinity to magical charms? We remember the Old High German 'Lorsch Bee Blessing', 'sizi, sizi, bina / sizi vilu stillo, wirki godes willon' – sit, sit, bee, sit completely still, do God's will. The swarming impulse again, as we recall: *Maya the Bee*, an impertinent bee, has hatched, the queen has lost her grip, and a little later Maya will leave the hive off her own bat. And we remember, once again, the beginning of *My Bee Year*: 'Absolute peace now prevails among the bees.' A simple sentence in a confident, relaxed tone; a clear observation, I said at the beginning – and yet there is an echo of that early medieval bee-charming, shifted to January for reasons of drama, when – as the lay reader cannot yet know at this point – swarming season is far away from the colony.

Lieselotte Gettert enchants not the colony but, at first, only her readers, and that without addressing us directly – this indirect form of address, speaking around corners, is a common magical procedure, aside from which, direct eye contact is widely regarded as a sign of aggression. Not an observation of nothing, as we now realise, but an entrance to the stage: the beekeeper speaks, her voice radiates authority, she demonstrates how the bees obey her every word, how the insects follow the will of God and the beekeeper. The voice calms us, as we experience how it can pacify bees.

It is likely every beekeeper's aim to encourage their bees' placidity and focus. However, even today's experts know little of the laws by which the honeybee lives. Every beekeeper has her preferences, like every bee colony. A panacea doesn't seem to exist. A wealth of bee behaviours can be predicted, yet individual colonies may develop completely differently – one colony perhaps reacting to human interventions in different ways every time; each situation a potential test for knowledge earned through experience.

Humans confronted with forces they barely understand: this is where art sets in. Entice, repel, tame, banish. We might ask whether the earliest manifestations of what we now call art were not all attempts to keep the animals around us in check. Whether they used divine or human forces to do so – what is perhaps most important is that they used non-animal means, tools that animals do not possess: symbols, depictions, human language.

Humankind itself moves only gradually to the fore in terms of artistic work, far removed from a central position for many generations. Scratchings, pattern formations, arrangements of found material in the landscape, colourings, rock paintings. A drawing in the Arana Cave at Bicorp, Valencia Province, created around 12,000 years before the Christian era, depicts a hole in a rock as a home to wild bees. A picture of a cavern within a cavern. The colony is agitated, two human honey-thieves climbing up a rope to reach it, and they'll rarely break the combs without reciting magical spells.

A direct path leads from apiculture to literature. Bees feed the young Jupiter – in a grotto. Later, they feed Pindar and Plato in their sleep. They lead their lives, as Virgil has it, under 'majestic laws,' and these are not only the laws of nature. According to Pliny, they have their own customs, prove themselves artistic creatures. Thus they are close to poets. And poets work in the way of bees, since 'they bring songs from honeyed fountains, culling them out of the gardens and dells of the Muses,' as Plato has Socrates say in his *Ion*.

On the cusp of the 19th and 20th centuries, in a time of grave change, apian imagery proves particularly productive in literature. Societies collapse, societies are created, the old queens appear tired, the workers grow agitated. Maurice Maeterlinck, as he attempts in *The Life of the Bee* to focus on the peace-loving nature of the honeybee. And Proust, that great admirer of Maeterlinck, as he imagines his favourite writer's garden, 'where the Virgil of Flanders – next to hives of straw painted in pink, yellow and tender blue which, upon entering, recall for us his preferred studies – has harvested such incomparable poetry.'

In the same year as Maya the Bee sets out in search of human contact in Bonsel's novel, we first meet a boy named

Marcel, in an advance publication from *In Search of Lost Time*, precisely on the first day of spring 1912. Exactly what type of creature are we dealing with, who throws himself upon the hawthorn hedge on leaving Combray? When referring to the olfactory character of hawthorn blossoms, most descriptions range from 'herring water' to 'carrion', and every plant guide hastens to add that such aromas exert a strong attraction for bees – Marcel, the narrator, speaks throughout of its 'fragrance'. Does he wish only to look at the blossoms, to inhale their 'fragrance', or is he pollinating them by throwing himself into the hedge? Not a child, you would think, but an insect, which – freshly coiffed in the morning and sporting a new hat – refuses to be made into a man. And tramples on his hair curlers by the hawthorn in a fit of rage. A remarkable coincidence, given that hair curlers are, to this day, a popular queen cage among beekeepers, used to prevent future subjects of a queen, newly brought into a colony, from gnawing at her legs.

A little later, Ossip Mandelstam takes a stand, with an almost desperate invocation of solitary bees against the overpowering image of the state-building bees as propagated by the Soviet Union. The subordination of the individual in the collective, regarded as a law of nature – the Central Committee seems to have read its Virgil rather fleetingly. In this situation, Mandelstam summons ancient Europe along with the poet bees: 'Take, from my palms, for joy, for ease / a little honey, a little sun, / that we may obey Persephone's bees,' he writes in 1920. Stalin himself keeps a few colonies at his dacha in Subalovo. When he confiscates an industrialist's country pile after the revolution in 1919, he immediately has an apiary built and buckwheat planted, for the honey, perhaps wishing the bees might feed him, too, in his sleep.

I began to immerse myself in *My Bee Year*, and soon bees colonised my dreams. Upon waking, I couldn't decide whether I'd written bee lines in my dream or taken care of my bees. When I – encouraged repeatedly, I was certain, by the author – started calculating over breakfast how much time four or ten colonies would cost me to keep over a year, when I weighed up the surprisingly light workload against the experience to be gained from dealing with bees, I realised just in time: I couldn't practice apiculture as a hobby, just as I can't write as a hobby. Were I to decide on beekeeping, my writing would soon be over.

An apiarist keeps hive cards over the year; notes on the development of individual colonies, the weather, the yield, on diseases and preventive measures. Every chapter in *My Bee Year* has a blank page at its end, on which readers can enter observations on their bees. In her foreword, Gettert points out that her *Working Calendar* can thus become a chronicle, over the years, in its readers' hands. Yes, bees and beekeeping are an old, well-stocked store of images for us poets. And beekeeping images are excellently suited to describe writing. This is what kept me from a life as an apiarist, enabled me to keep writing: the two activities are too similarly structured for me to pursue both.

How observation and imagination interpermeate. The mental immersion, the intervention in another world that exists even without me; a world I know I will never quite understand. The tremendous intensity – all senses are challenged, every nerve addressed, as I enter into an interaction, be it with a bee colony or with language. The slightest distraction on my part can disturb the fabric so severely that all subsequent work is in vain. There are routines, rehearsed motions, to be sure – but I must always go to work with sharp eyes, must examine colony and language anew every time. And every solution I find may have no validity for anyone else, indeed, may soon no longer be of any help to me.

Bees react to their keeper, but they don't know the beekeeper. So too, language. I handle it, I steer it a little way, it comes towards me, and in the next instant slips away again. I think I'm familiar with language, and yet I must always be aware: language doesn't know me. Just like the bee colony, it retains its mystery; it lives and shifts according to its own laws. And like the beekeeper, I can't afford to be sentimental – in the worst case, I must sulphur.

Beekeeping, I know this now, is writing without text. I suspect a beekeeper might say the same, perhaps in other words. As I write, I speak to myself, my larynx in constant motion. And I am certain Lieselotte Gettert also murmurs to her bees while she works.

VII

Language broadens the world. Walking the dog in this country unreceptive to linguistic magic; a place that distrusts the magic of language – walking along the banks of the Elbe in Dresden decade after decade with an elegant Afghan hound that loses nothing of its paraded dignity even in the wildest chase; and calling out its name, since it is growing ever smaller on the horizon, making comrades and philistines alike hold their ears as the name echoes across the narrow Elbe Valley: 'Eciya!'

Or: 'Mikado!'

Or: 'Gangadhao!'

Or: 'Nepomuk!'

Up in Weisser Hirsch: Baron Manfred von Ardenne. Below, belting across fields with billowing fur: Eciya vom Isishof, Nepomuk vom Paradiespark. The aristocratic 'vom' in these names refers to nothing more than a breeding line, and yet Gangadhao must have been aware of her noblesse, having once rattled some uninvited visitors, sniffing around with sustained growling and baring of teeth to such an extent that the Stasi preferred to break off their house search altogether.

131

'One has to know how to lose – with grandeur,' says the owner of Eciya, Mikado and Gangadhao, now present only in photographs and portraits. At some point in the course of the same afternoon, I ask her the names of her Afghan hounds, their leather leashes dangling in the dusk of the cloakroom. As I touch one of the now-brittle collars with my right hand, I can almost feel my left hand being sniffed by a canine muzzle, as if it were time to walk down to the Elbe.

*

Thirteen years that goldfish lived in the aquarium beside her bed, my friend tells me; far longer than its two one-eyed co-habitants. It would wake the mistress of the house in the morning with gentle plashing, and when she ironed, it would watch and swim back and forth, following the motion of her hand. It would lie perfectly still on her hand and watch her when she took it out of the tank and put it in a bucket to clean the aquarium. At the end, it could no longer swim, would float with its mouth to the bottom, and the last time she lifted it out of the water it gave her a final long look in the eye.

Little red goldfish in an aquarium. Visiting the former Stasi premises on Bautzner Strasse, I notice an empty glass tank in the anteroom to the basement cell wing known by the name of 'Fox's Den'. As was commonly the case in Eastern European institutions, they kept ornamental fish here too. I don't know whether sunbleaks from the Moritzburg ponds once swam behind the glass, or sticklebacks, which – depending on their hormonal mood – seem at times to blend in with their diffuse green background, at times to defend their territory in contrasting colours, viewing nearly everything and everyone – even a human finger – as an enemy, attacking with lightning speed, repelling to the point of utter exhaustion.

No, I consider, as the memorial guide explains how we're unable to visit the actual 'Fox's Den', because it is now part of the vocational training centre in the front part of the building; no, they can't have been banal sticklebacks, sunbleaks or other native dabbling fish. The interior logic of an NKVD, a Ministry of State Security, an Office of National Security demands a reliable dash of colour in this place. A bleak, windowless room is far better suited to giving the new inmate an idea of the level of bleakness that awaits him in the adjacent cell wing if the guards feed goldfish in front of him.

Was this aquarium at the entrance to the 'Fox's Den' a secret, back then? Did word of its existence get around the city? When they lead you down a basement corridor, at the end of which a door opens onto a view of a few shiny red goldfish standing out almost painfully from the grey surroundings, you know you're only a few steps away from the dark cell.

But who could have given anyone that warning? An eye witness. A Stasi man. Or a broken, possibly turncoat ex-prisoner.

At the beginning of December 1989, a rumour went around Dresden that the KGB was holding prisoners in what were called 'water cells' in a tunnel beneath the Elbe, as Vladimir Putin tells it. People also suspected a 'water cell' in the Stasi basement.

A hallucination? Deliberate disinformation spread by secret service men mingling with the demonstrators? The enraged mob demanded to see the water cells. They were never found, neither in the basement nor under the Elbe.

Walking on the bank below the former Stasi headquarters at the end of August 2002, when the Elbe retired to its bed after flooding, we discovered, between plastic sheeting and branches and drinks cartons, a pair of pale red patches in the dingy mud of a puddle: two slightly injured, exhausted-looking goldfish.

*

A little red sign on my windscreen: 'PARKING OFFENDER. Please leave this parking space or purchase a permit. Information on fees is available from the property management company. The caretaker.'

We've come to visit a friend who recently moved into this estate on Bautzner Strasse. In the old days, the place was inhabited solely by Stasi employees. Yes, it was only a few yards to work every day; yes, the location wasn't bad, with the woods and stream behind the building; yes, the newbuilds were comfortable; and yes, there was no need for rumours in this closed society; there was no gossip about what kind of work the neighbour might do. All plausible reasons, all tiny promises to draw 'their own people' together in one place. Outside, in the city, in the 1980s, they apparently feared for the safety of every single employee; safety that was far better guaranteed under the watchful eyes of their colleagues.

These days, you hear Russian here, hear languages from other former Soviet republics. All the more remarkable that on turning into the area secured with a 24-hour access barrier, the guest is greeted by huge hand-made signs, every inch of them covered in sentences in not entirely orthographically correct German with numerous exclamation marks, pointing out: private land, no parking, parking permits, parking fees, and so on. Similar signs can be found at almost every car park in Western Europe, we thought, unworried on the way to see our friend, since we were visitors, after all.

Even the sight of a man standing broad-legged on the pavement at the other end of the block didn't unsettle me; you see men like that in tracksuit pants and sweaty T-shirts all over the world, and he did at least watch us wave to our friend as we got out of the car, while he waved back from his open window – I wouldn't have classed myself as a criminal 'parking interloper' intent on surreptitiously stealing a parking space.

A little red sticker on my passenger window. 'WARNING. This vehicle is blocked by a wheel clamp. Do not attempt to drive. Removal can only be carried out by the caretaker.'

Our friend shrugs. The same procedure every time. He dials the telephone number on the sticker; in 10 minutes, he's told, the caretaker will have time to remove the wheel clamp. It's not worth thinking about the legal basis of his approach – as far as I know, even touching a vehicle is classed as wilful damage in Germany. We wait. In ten minutes, the caretaker demonstrates that we do not have free dominion over our time. Our time is in his hands. He savours his power, for 10, 15, 18 long minutes.

A little red-faced man by the guinea pig run. While we were smoking a cigarette on our friend's balcony, enjoying the view of the stream and the woods and hearing the guinea pigs in their fenced-in run on the grass detect whether they were being eyed by a harmless bird or a dangerous one, an elderly man came past.

He was picking up paper from the grass with a grabber; he turned to us, said hello, and we greeted him back. Our friend exchanged a few words with him and made a joke, telling him not to mistake the patchy guinea pigs for rubbish and put them in his plastic bucket. A mid-morning chat between neighbours, then the man was gone again, and our friend told us the names his daughters had given the guinea pigs.

When the caretaker appears, he is not – as I would have suspected – the man in the tracksuit pants who examined us earlier, but that elderly gent with whom we'd held a balcony conversation.

Everything must have gone according to a precise plan. The tracksuit-pants man informs the rubbish-grabber. The rubbish-grabber waits a moment until the door closes behind us, then he inserts the laminated 'parking offender' sign behind the windscreen wiper. He does a round of the building; assures himself we'll be staying longer than a few minutes with our friend – we're smoking on the balcony – makes an effort not to appear too hurried, bucket and grabber in hand; disappears at the end of the building; walks back in the opposite direction on the other side; adheres the sticker to the passenger window and finally affixes the wheel clamp. Now all he has to do is conceal himself somewhere and await the telephone call.

To quote the Stasi: 'Please don't talk nonsense, otherwise we'll have to use violence.'

On the adjacent plot there was once a small annex where interrogations took place. It had the internal name of 'Witch's Hut'.

The floor of the arrest cells was painted red.

I've never faced an active Stasi employee; the end of the Stasi is half my lifetime ago; and fox's dens, witch's huts and red-painted cell floors will always remain outside the bounds of my imagination, despite impressive descriptions by people who tried, kitted out only with a coarse blanket, to sleep on such floors. Which the guard prevented.

And yet, as we leave the estate through the 24-hour barrier, I feel a mix of impotence, lack of comprehension and rage, as

136

though someone had just made me realise: that defunct world will continue to exist until the end of time.

*

Sleep deprivation, the technical term: 'white torture'.

*

Little pink patch of wall. I don't know what efforts I'd have undertaken to accommodate myself in a closed world without going mad. Stuck in the smallest of spaces, we must learn to stagger them into so many smaller spaces that they seem impenetrable.

Jean Cocteau and Louis Aragon show how that can work, without being properly aware of it, in one of the oddest books published in the second half of the 20th century, *Conversations on the Dresden Gallery*.

The French edition is from 1957, yet it doesn't consist, as you might expect, of conversations following a visit to Dresden, where Cocteau and Aragon would have inspected the artworks returned from the Soviet Union in 1956, capturing their immediate impressions on tape so that those Western European art lovers for whom a trip to the GDR wasn't possible could get an impression of the Painting Gallery.

The two of them hold their long, enthusiastic conversation in Paris. They apparently don't even dream they might need to leave Paris to appreciate the Old Masters. To see them. To enter a state of euphoria. Cocteau and Aragon look at catalogue illustrations, picture postcards and colour reproductions on a light box. Bear in mind that in the art printing process, colours are mere approximations of the original, in fact more like proxies, and the effect of the specific format is absent. Working after a reproduction – the rest, the decisive rest, is up to the imagination. Thus, the two men put themselves in a situation in which every Dresdener had until recently found themselves, even if they may have had a memory of the paintings, had they known them from the time before their disappearance into secret Soviet archives.

A staggered, multiply diverted perspective: the art print of the photograph of the painting – and the imagined way back through this staggered world, without having to rebel against the two-dimensionality of what is known as flat products. For the imagination inserts trap doors even into a world of height times width.

Thus, Cocteau talks himself into a colour high while reflecting on a black-and-white illustration of Canaletto's *Campo San Giacomo di Rialto, Venice*. 'That Venetian square,' he says, 'that part in the shade there, and under the arcades, and that pink wall,' Cocteau hesitates for a moment, 'for I'm sure it must be pink,' before he casts a brief glance at the human figures: 'And look, down there, some painters arguing.'

What are these painters the painter has put in the picture arguing over – perhaps a little patch of pink wall? Subservient Aragon has a colour illustration at hand, and the two writers soon lean over the light box. Cocteau sees himself confirmed, the wall is in fact pink, and lets that luminous colour impression lead him into the literary sphere: 'It reminds me of the pink house by Vermeer, which Proust's Bergotte was gazing at as he died.'

A footnote explains 'a curious color-blind fault of memory' that befell Cocteau: He, 'having imagined the wall in the Canaletto to be pink,' in his mind's eye then 'imagined the wall was pink in Vermeer's *View of the Town of Delft* in the Hague Museum, though' – the note adds for lay readers on the topic of Proust and Vermeer – 'in fact it is yellow.'

'In fact' – marvellous. Not only does Cocteau replace a yellow with a pink patch of wall in his imagination; the footnote also replaces an imaginary patch of wall with a 'factual' one. For Proust, after all, invented the 'little patch of yellow wall' in the *View of Delft*, so as to have Bergotte die at the sight of it.

In fact? Hurrah for the twofold, twofold imaginary, yellow and pink patch of wall. In contrast, the constant, the tiring, essentially unrealistic insistence on 'authenticity'. Those who wish to nail everything down to 'authenticity', those who willingly let themselves be nailed down to 'authenticity', stand and fall with this very 'authenticity'. Thus the world shrinks down to the head of that nail.

Those of us who have held books in our hands since childhood develop, over time, a certain optical, in this case even tactile sensitivity, which leads us on the tracks of a book's origins before we've read a word. I sense that my *Conversations on the Dresden Gallery* must originate from the GDR, my fingertips tell me so, as do my eyes. I recognise it by the coarse blue-grey linen binding. The book states, 'Stuttgart: Belser 1981', yet the printing location is clearly noted to be Leipzig.

Just like its mental space, the geographical space is staggered: a book by two authors in Paris who talk about the Old Masters as though on an extended tour of the gallery, and then the copies of this book are exported from Leipzig to West Germany. Was there also an East German edition? Could a Dresdener – staggering in reverse – read the conversations about reproductions of paintings, only to then go to the museum and compare the two writers' descriptions and impressions against the originals?

'Compare against the original' – yet another negative spirit of the petty world lying in wait.

*

A painted, a photographed, and a living dog snatch at history. The painted dog hung for a while in the cafeteria of Dresden's New Masters Gallery located on Brühl's Terrace. Those who knew about the picture could also spot it through the glass door while on tours during exhibition openings – the cafeteria is closed in the evenings – in a corner beside the counter. Fifty by fifty centimetres, oil on canvas, grey in grey, painted after a photograph in 1967.

During the day, visitors will have passed by this painted dog without paying it further attention, the way we might pass by a living dog lying at its mistress's feet under a coffee-house table. Unless it was a celebrity's dog. But no one expects a Gerhard Richter in a museum café.

The portrait of a Cairn terrier, a breed bred since the beginning of the 20th century. It takes its name from the layered stone pyramids in the Scottish Highlands; the landmarks or commemorative markers near which the dog might put its love of hunting and digging to use while tracking down foxes, badgers, otters. The dramatic colour changes that a Cairn terrier's coat can pass through before it reaches adulthood are a mystery to breeders to this day. Similar terriers can be found in pictures from as long ago as the 15th century. And initially, it seemed this painting might be effortlessly included in the long tradition of pet portraits, in a gallery that hangs famous racehorses alongside outstanding hunting dogs; companions not only for hunting but for life. The picture is called *Jockel*, as is its subject.

But Gerhard Richter painted this animal as though portraying a person. The face fills the centre of the canvas; the shaggy fur extends to the edges; we see the dog up close, the shiny nose apparently touching the picture's surface. Without meaning to, the observer seeks Jockel's gaze, seeks to attract his gaze, but he looks unswervingly past us. Assuming the photograph it was painted after was not an enlarged section or shot using a zoom, the dog would have to have been very familiar with the photographer to let them get so close without being restrained.

The live Cairn terrier by the name of Jockel is a dog I know only anecdotally. He belonged to the art historian Will Grohmann, whose monographs on Klee and Kandinsky are standard works to this day; the same Grohmann who opens the door of Ida Bienert's private collection, on Samuel Beckett's visit to Dresden in February 1937. Will Grohmann is 50 at the time, and always eager to see new, unconventional, non-conformist art. Or an art enthusiast and young writer from Ireland, who receives a rejection of his *Murphy* manuscript during his days in Dresden – the book with the now famous opening sentence: 'The sun shone, having no alternative, on the nothing new.'

The Nazis' travelling exhibition 'Degenerate Art' is not opened until after Beckett's departure; at the New Masters, they tell him he can't view the already removed modernist works in the depot either. At Ida Bienert's, he admires Kandinsky's *Improvisation* (*Dreamy*). He receives Will Grohmann's catalogue of the collection as a gift – but he is told to take utmost care on the rest of his German tour not to let anyone cast a glance at this index of hidden pictures.

Grohmann introduces Beckett into Dresden society, Dresden's art society, and Beckett thanks him, in his discreet way, by mentioning Grohmann in 1945 in 'The World and the Trousers' as one of the greatest art critics. He recalls how Grohmann established Kandinsky's 'Mongolian lines'.

After 1945, Will Grohmann learns that his idea of new perspectives of the world – as art, and only art, can construct – is incompatible with the new art doctrine. 'The sun shone, having no alternative, on the nothing new.' He leaves Dresden for West Germany, Berlin. And dies, on the threshold to another new

141

age, on 6 May 1968 – only weeks after the assassination attempt on the activist Rudi Dutschke, as students erect barricades in West Berlin and Paris. Jockel was Grohmann's last dog.

Jockel, a gesture of friendship by Gerhard Richter for Will Grohmann, is not among the best-known works of this painter who processed the fully photographed world with his brush – for which the world takes revenge by fully photographing Richter's works. The curious would seek *Jockel* in vain in catalogues; the painting doesn't even appear in lists of Richter's collected works until it passes from private ownership into the New Masters' collection in the early 1990s.

Jockel, I know anecdotally, survived his owner. In 1970, he is a witness to a covertly unfolding story, only to disappear from view, like his portrait, almost abandoned. In that year, Will Grohmann's sister-in-law from Dresden wants to visit her younger sister, Grohmann's widow, but on arrival in Munich finds her dead. Having studied the train timetable in preparation for her suicide, Annemarie Grohmann calculated in advance which person would be the first to see her corpse. More than 30 years later, when her elder sister and I are looking at old photographs together, I dare not ask where the dog was at that moment – I get the impression that that moment still feels too fresh. While big sister was on her way, little sister already knew there would be no reunion.

The live Jockel was placed in the care of two elderly ladies in Munich; there could be no question of taking him with her to Dresden. And there, all trace of him is lost. Gerhard Richter's *Jockel* remains in the West until it appears unanticipated on the wall of a museum café in the New Masters, some day after the end of the Cold War. No one knows where the photograph on which the portrait was based might be.

Even from the painted animal, we expect some kind of stirring; a reaction to us, his observers. Not that the dog looks tired, the way his front paws are resting under his muzzle. Jockel, a dog once surrounded by modern art. The alert eyes. The centre of his attention is slightly to the left of the picture and of us. Be it that he's immersed in a moment, be it that he's just about to leap up to examine the object of his interest more closely, to follow a scent.

A terrier wants to dig.

*

'Resumption of the *White Boards* of the sixties with newly developed material in various sizes,' Wilhelm Müller notes under the heading 'from 1986' in his list of works dated 10 June 1989, one of his few written testaments intended for the public. We can only assume that these *White Boards* are the works described to me in detail four years after Müller's death in November 1999. According to that description, the painter had one day come up with the idea to make a series of carefully wrought boards in a format of approximately 25 by 35 centimetres; nothing but wonderfully treated surfaces in an even white-grey tone, without a trace of stroke or structure. There is evidence of at least two boards, yet I couldn't say whether they are a pair or a series, and as with so many of Wilhelm Müller's works, it is unclear who owns them or where they're held. It is said Wilhelm Müller was proud of these white surfaces, but the friends to whom he left them, visual artists like himself, were apparently partly disappointed, partly dismayed.

Provided only with a vivid description in words and gestures, what made me take note were the dimensions indicated – for these 25 by 35 centimetres correspond remarkably to the dimensions of the paper used in Japan for classical calligraphy, *hanshi*, which varies slightly in height between 33 and 35, in width between 24 and 26 centimetres. Thus, Wilhelm

143

Müller would have begun by processing a piece of cardboard or hardboard to utter inconspicuousness, treating what we are accustomed to viewing as a base with such perseverance and accuracy that the applied paint appears once again as a base, to then, in the final step, make a landscape format out of the Japanese portrait format.

Fiction has it that a week before Wilhelm Müller's 56th birthday, on 12 March 1974, representatives of the Czechoslovakian state knock at the door of the deceased Baron von Utz in Prague to call in his side of a longstanding bargain: Utz, the titular protagonist of Bruce Chatwin's novel, was assured that the private collection of Meissen porcelain hoarded in his home would remain untouched during his lifetime, but in return, the baron was obliged not to take the rare pieces out of the country, so that the entire collection could fall to the state after his death.

As nobody opens the door, the state obtains access to the apartment. It is empty. In the display cabinets, only blank patches in a fine layer of dust testify to the recent presence of the Utz collection's valuable Meissen pieces.

What Chatwin, a porcelain appreciator himself and employed at Sotheby's before he became a writer, invented here is based on a genuine case: at the end of the 1990s, the lost collection of the novel's inspiration Rudolf Just came to light and was auctioned off in December 2001.

This story occurs to me when I hear of an episode that must have taken place shortly before Wilhelm Müller's death. With the end of the GDR, there's suddenly a market for him, an artist who previously allowed himself to devote months at a time to a single sheet, years to one object. He used to give his work away, and now he has customers. An auction house is also interested in Müller's collection of art objects from various cultures, in his own and others' works in his possession. However, when Wilhelm Müller receives a visit from an auction-house employee, that man – presumably prepared to evaluate and perhaps even appraise pictures and sculptures – finds largely empty rooms. Before the market finally obtains access, Müller has got rid of his collection. I cannot judge the atmosphere during that meeting in the empty apartment. Perhaps secret triumph flashes in Wilhelm Müller's eyes, perhaps it is simply onerous for him; his gaze marked by a pain that no one, no friend, no doctor, no auctioneer could take from him.

'We say nothing,' Wilhelm Müller is said to have responded when asked, of the Quaker community meetings in Dresden: 'What do you say there?' Be it that the question seemed too forward to him at the time, be it that Müller was also an artist of silence – what his motivations were when he began a conversation, avoided a conversation or abruptly ended a conversation, even people who'd known him for many years couldn't say, especially in his later life.

Though I don't recall the occasion, I do know the two of us met shortly after I moved from Cologne to Dresden, presumably in the summer of 1996. Our conversation flourished immediately. We meet three or at most four more times, which I experience as tremendously intense and remember vividly. Perhaps, I think, meeting Müller was my first, defining experience of the East. He lends me three books: *Fremd unter meinesgleichen*, the memoirs of the Jewish Dresdener Helmut Eschwege, *Im Auftrag der Kirche*, Johannes Rau's memories of the last two years of the GDR, and Robert Lowry's novel *Casualty*.

His day job grants him the greatest possible freedom in his artistic work, Müller says; otherwise we hardly mention his work as a stomatologist in our conversation. That he ascribes his precision in the use of silverpoint to his many years of handling dental instruments, I find out only later. His knowledge of art history occupies far more time; his early interest in East Asia;

145

his collecting beginning in the second half of the 1950s, when he worked at the polyclinic in Welzow. He talks of rugs, on which he is an expert, as on porcelain. Objects rest in his hand – the haptic, the material aspect plays a major role. Objects that pass through his hands: on several occasions he swaps objects, entire collections with which he has lived for a few years, for others, or simply gives them away because they no longer speak to him.

From the spring of 1999, we keep postponing our next meeting – there's so much to do at the moment, let's wait for quieter times, and I put that comment down to exhibition preparations, naturally enough, but Müller has apparently long been occupied with something else. He has handed in notice on his studio, is dispersing his collection bit by bit, giving away, selling or returning works to the artists. Then he clears his apartment and enquires after a burial plot in Loschwitz Cemetery. I don't get an opportunity to return his borrowed books, and our conversation breaks off abruptly.

Of course, it is no deep insight that Wilhelm Müller adopted the dimensions of *hanshi* for his own boards: he is not only a connoisseur of the material, he also particularly enjoys working on Japanese paper, uses Japanese multicoloured pencil and, since his studio is only usable during the summer months, creates his *Japanese Circus* at home in the winters from 1984 to 1986, having focused in the winters since 1978 on *Playing with Silverpoint*.

Nonetheless, this moment illuminates a basic trait of his works: despite all their clarity, restriction, patency, there is always something for the observer to discover. Not in the sense that they are pictorial puzzles, but by the observer grasping their structure and then getting caught on a detail, one of their essential elements: for instance, in the case of these boards, the centimetre measurements. I don't know whether Müller really did once formulate the following in conversation: 'But I experience intensely only the tiny feelings of the tiniest things. This must come from my love of the futile or perhaps my passion for detail.' Should that be the case, however, then he would have been quoting statements that also appear in Fernando Pessoa's *Book of Disquiet*.

Besides that, the evenly grey-white surfaces must also be seen before a different background; there is a second contextual reference. Carl Rade, whose 'student grandson' Müller regarded himself as, is said, when his students once helped him move house, to have remarked that a number of tightly wrapped packages were absolutely off limits. The helpers carried the mysterious items to the van as instructed, without looking inside. One package, however, fell to the floor; the wrapping ripped open, and what appeared was nothing more than a stack of white-primed sheets of cardboard. By giving his white surfaces to students and admirers of Rade, Wilhelm Müller not only measures the quality of his own surfaces against those of his role model, as if competing, but also re-discloses the master's secret in an earnest yet playful tribute.

The inconspicuous detail, the superficially insignificant: Müller possessed an apparently unremarkable scrap of paper from the late Hermann Glöckner, who accepted Müller as a student in the 1960s, granting him access to his studio. That privilege applied only as long as the teacher believed he was dealing with a dentist, not with a colleague who might work out what simple foundations, for instance paper-folding, his own work was built. Certainly, that scrap of paper was not a key piece of Glöckner's oeuvre, and yet on the basis of its few lines, perhaps some shading, Müller could prove: here, Glöckner has pursued the question of the minimum of creative input to turn a torn-off piece of paper into a stand-alone form.

Carl Rade's white secret, Hermann Glöckner's folding secret: Wilhelm Müller candidly passes on his secrets, the results of years of exploring his material. For all our enthusiasm for skill, for well-wrought pieces, it remains clear that the mystery cannot be exhausted in the manufacturing method; the mystery is contained in the work as it hangs on the wall or stands on the table. The method may be revealed, but not the outcome.

At our last meeting, we stand by the window in his apartment, looking west. He wouldn't want to do without this view, he tells me, this glazed façade, even though he doesn't think the flat here in the GDR-built block on Prager Strasse is particularly good; it's small, and he works mainly in the shower now, only with silverpoint. His eyesight is rapidly deteriorating, not that he talks about it. His back is gone; he'll soon be incapable of walking. He doesn't talk about his high blood pressure, his illness and the pain.

When this building, where he's lived for almost 30 years, was constructed, the architects built upon a just-cleared surface. By structuring the void, they made Dresden's centre empty once again. When the two of us look down from one of the top floors onto the right-angled paving stones; onto the roof of the pavilion; the row of shops opposite; onto exposed concrete and fountains, not even the Lenin statue is left standing in the pedestrian zone beneath us, no longer keeping an eye on the station as he did until a few years ago.

During the night of 4 October 1989, Wilhelm Müller watched – first at the station and then from his window – as this empty space filled with people. The events of that night and the subsequent days moved him deeply, as he wrote on postcards to friends and now tells me too. When the police bludgeoned those who sought to get close to the trains transporting the so-called exit-willing from Prague to West Germany, routed via

Dresden, he tells me, the demonstrators, the curious onlookers, the passers-by backed off, but at some point they stopped letting themselves be provoked into retaliating that violence as the state wished them to do. That courage to fully surrender themselves impressed Müller, a radical rejecter of violence, a Quaker.

Now, however, we stare out at a deserted space.

Surfaces divided at right angles, a red line, strips of shadow, shining silver, as though we are looking at a piece by Müller himself. But these aren't hardboard sheets – no Alusil has been sprayed here, no line drawn in minutely with silver ink. It is the ground on which, on a deserted November night 10 years after the events at Dresden's main station, the painter Wilhelm Müller will lie.

What remains is an empty flat. Gone are Müller's skills, preferences, learnings, pictures and words, everything contained – like so much in this now barely recognisable city – only in hands and heads. Like Wilhelm Müller's precisely wrought, evenly white-grey boards, which I can only see in my mind's eye.

*

When I attempt to remember 9 November 1989, I see not the suddenly permeable border fortifications in Berlin, not crowds of people or stalling convoys of Wartburgs and Trabants. Instead, what comes to mind is my own first car.

The dealer from whom I bought the midnight-blue Fiat 127 in the urban blight between Cologne and Neuss during the early autumn of 1989 ran a garage in one of the trading estates, which was characterised by round-the-clock busyness and yet still appeared dead. Here a tow-truck with its engine running on the side of the road, there the illuminated window of a haulage office, in the background the clink of metal on metal from an open workshop, yet not a soul to be seen. I would have been highly unlikely to set out unprompted into this purgatory, in search of a sign saying LICHTHORN.

Lichthorn, a Sorbian mechanic, was the man who repaired the cars of the Cologne region's Sorbian minority, and since the father of my girlfriend at the time was Sorbian, I, too, was sent to his workshop, where there were always a few used cars on the forecourt waiting for new owners. The price for the Fiat 127, belonging to a distant relative from Upper Lusatia, a woman known to have been a careful owner, was negotiated from Sorb to Sorb by telephone. Buying cars, it appeared, involved old horse-trading tenets.

Via these family links, despite having no particular mental associations with either the GDR or eastern Germany, I became immersed in a sphere new to me; understood something of the simultaneous existence of different worlds, of invisible borderlines contained neither on the map nor in ideological handbooks. Be it only in the form of that patronising attitude towards East Germans of which there was no lack in the West, even before November 1989. On one occasion, a waiter to my girlfriend's mother: 'Poor girl, did you only get a boy from over there?'

Almost 30 years had passed since the Wall was built – and still people had to reckon with that kind of comment. A situation in which those who won't succumb to self-pity become stoics. No wonder, too, that the migration of the father's family, from the area around Kamenz, was told not as a tale of fear and flight, but as a series of adventurous journeys: in the days before the Berlin Wall, one sister went on a trip to the Rhineland – and felt no compulsion to return to the rural structures of Upper Lusatia. So they sent a brother after her to fetch her back home – but he, too, liked life in Cologne. Whereupon the next sister sallied forth – and so on, until all the siblings were reunited in the Rhineland even before the border was sealed. Not until

13 August 1961 did the tone of the story change. After that date, when it came to bringing their parents across the newly built wall to the West, the travellers' tale became an exit story. And that was the end of it.

It was thanks to my car, with which I was very happy even though it needed frequent repairs, that I didn't witness the events around 9 November 1989 solely from my West German perspective. The next generation of Sorbs now set out for the Rhine, perhaps for a few weeks, perhaps forever. Every time I turned up at Lichthorn's garage, I saw new faces. Another distant young relative or a son of a former neighbour had turned up, drawn to where he could tinker with VWs. A shuttle transit between the Rhineland and Upper Lusatia was rapidly established, accommodation and jobs arranged for the new arrivals. For self-taught mechanics from Bautzen, Kamenz or Dresden, the oil pan and indicators of my midnight-blue Fiat 127 were a welcome test – he who passed got to make a broken-down Golf roadworthy again. I watched all this from the sidelines, but also from close up. What was going on in the heads of the emigrated and the newly arrived Sorbs, however, I don't know.

My girlfriend's father reacted to his internal conflict between scepticism and euphoria with 'objectivity'. And viewed the events across the border in the form of television pictures, which he commentated in terse words. You had to stay objective, he claimed – this meant nothing but a warning to himself not to expect too much, in view of the holidaymakers escaped from Hungary, the Monday demonstrations and the border opening. He remained the stoic he had become in the West. Thinking about when he first told me about leaving the East, however, I realise it might have been at exactly that time. His brother, meanwhile, was the first to transport a repaired VW Golf to the East – his internal commotion was transformed into external migration. Today, I see the brother and his son among the participants of the annual mounted procession, when the Sorbian Easter Riders are welcomed to the monastery court-yard in Panschwitz-Kuckau.

The family never used the words 'East Germans', let alone 'GDR citizens'. Nor did I ever hear a term like *Volk*. Possibly, the soon routine Sorbian back-and-forth between East and West led me to the – albeit only semi-conscious – idea that the area between Dresden and Bautzen had not been part of the GDR, but a kind of exterritorial region.

In November 1989, I regularly drove east along the A4, an autobahn once intended to cross the entire country, to my university town of Siegen. I sat in a dark-blue car that almost resembled a Trabant from a distance, with Cologne number plates, while cars with GDR number plates came towards me: a brief phase when using your horn was not understood as an insult.

Everything seemed near and very far at once. I learned place names I'd never heard before, words that have since remained beads on a long string for me, impossible to pry out of their adjacencies: *Krabat*, for instance, *Kroate*, *Krawatte*. A place name like Klotzsche, a name like Ottendorf, or Okrilla – nothing could have sounded more unreal, back then in November 1989, but had someone come along and said: Let's go to Ottendorf-Okrilla, I'd have leapt into the car without hesitation.

I remember June 2007, when we were combing Dresden for studio space and viewing disused factories, unlettable offices, depreciable property investments unaired since 1990. On one occasion, a manager's office with an upholstered door, three-piece suite, expansive desk, a resubmission folder and a telephone at arm's reach, one chair tilted towards the glazed façade as though the boss had just popped to the toilet in the middle of a modernisation effort. Another time, a long room with a view of the slopes down to the Elbe, drawing us involuntarily to the light, behind us stacks of boxes and binders up to the ceiling. They'd needed storage space, the caretaker told us, but presumably he no longer knew himself what had been stored there, to what purpose. I didn't want to know either. In my 12th year in Dresden, spaces like that no longer had an aura of enchantment.

One hot morning, we had an appointment in the north of the city, far out in a wooded industrial area with garages, scrap dealers, computer companies. Aside from a few security guards in imaginary uniforms smoking on the side of the road outside a security firm, there was no one to be seen. No blight like between Cologne and Neuss; here, you could imagine yourself to be driving around a never-ending forestscape, and yet the area seemed no more alive. When a fence blocked our way, we knew we'd missed the correct turn-off. Beyond scrubland, we spotted the airport runway. It was as though the countless pines and birches there had only been planted to create a sense of disorientation and hide the buildings, in which the first and only German passenger jet had been developed in the 1950s, though the prototype later smashed to pieces in a nearby field during a test flight.

An accommodating custodian then led us through the side wing of a simple, solidly bricked building, former workshops, an administration section and training rooms; unlocked room after room; suggested knocking out walls, repairing sanitary installations, already excited for new tenants. We might possibly have haggled the rent down to 75 cents per square metre – and still: no, I couldn't do it, I choked at the thought of spending longer than necessary on these premises.

Afterwards, we sat on a rotting park bench in a small patch of green, where the employees from the surrounding buildings might once have spent their lunch breaks. We considered pros and cons: the reasonable rent, a lease beginning the next month, versus the small, barred windows, the low slatted ceiling. I saw in my mind's eye the plastic channels above the skirting boards, varying indecisively between eggshell and grey, intended to conceal the wiring added at a later date. I saw the carpeting, grubby, faded. It was the carpeting that I knew, that made me uncomfortable, against which I raised an internal objection: No, there can be no way back.

Back – where? Without thinking, I would have said: Back to the GDR, I can't stand that GDR atmosphere any more. For me, who grew up in the West, it has lost the allure of the unknown, and all that remains is the aspect that accompanied friends from the East throughout their youth: oppressive plainness. As if I'd spent my own days inside such spaces in GDR times. An attack of exaggerated empathy? Or was I coming to an end of my own 1990s, in which I'd explored abandoned eastern spaces with great curiosity? I felt no more melancholia, only desolation. But why was my reaction so extreme?

We had long since stopped talking about renting a studio in Klotzsche by the time it occurred to me that that carpeting and those cable channels were by no means relics of the GDR, but traces of the first renovations carried out after 1989, in expectation of exacting new tenants. Tenants primarily from the West, who felt the need for familiar interiors. Thus, the East was flooded with simultaneously luxurious and practical fittings, as found in West German spaces during the previous decade. I hadn't flinched at an image of the GDR. I saw myself planted inside an image I'd left far behind me, temporally and geographically, and I'd flinched at a memory of the world whence I'd come.

I knew the carpeting of the Rhineland, I knew the carpeting of Vienna and England, I knew it well. Grey, grey-green or formerly foxy-red; now only salmony-orange carpeting wherever I set foot. I knew the radiator-staled air. The old West. As if nothing had changed over two decades. As if I were still the same person as in my early twenties. I did not, I realised, want to go back there.

I first landed at Dresden-Klotzsche Airport on 9 June 1991. Perhaps I could have seen the fields at Ottendorf-Okrilla below me during our descent, from which – in a different time, a different world – the smashed remains of a jet plane had been collected up, on 4 March 1959, a date that lay barely further back for me at that moment than 9 November 1989.

When I attempt to remember that night of 9 November 1989, I see myself sitting in a Cologne cinema in the summer of that year, at the West German premiere of Tim Burton's *Batman*. The film is set mainly in the dark of night, but I don't think of *Batman* because of the images; I don't think of a city in the grip of dark powers where the sun no longer rises, or of the hero, an ordinary citizen by day who dons a bat costume at night to make the world a better place; instead, I hear a command: 'Trust me.'

I hear Jack Nicholson playing the Joker – a white-painted counterpart to Egon Krenz, the former politician whose tanned skin colour astounds me to this day, standing out almost obscenely against the cheese-skinned Eastern Bloc cadre. As though, while the others squatted in their bunkers, he had been strolling on the Crimea, or – part of the sinister powers-that-be in a dark land – spending an hour a day on a sunbed.

'Trust me.' That short phrase crops up every few minutes in *Batman*; by the end every character has said it at least once. The audience at the midnight showing crowed with delight whenever the two syllables punctuated the largely predictable plot, for in the world of Gotham City they signal nothing but scheming for mischief, a plot underway, a rescue plan about to go wrong, a marker for utter distrust.

And simultaneously, it is as if the director and screenwriters were firing out an invitation to the audience, out of the film, from the mouth of every single character: 'We know you believe neither in Gotham City nor in men in black catsuits who save the world under cover of night – but we ask you to follow us, just this once.' How far must the direct effect of fiction have come if it requires such desperate requests for its acceptance by the audience – or, the opposite: if it can permit itself such break-outs from the closed circle of the fictional film world?

That fiction must always substantiate itself, that it comes about only by questioning itself, seemed to go without saying, in the West, at the end of the 1980s. Tim Burton, however, whose films have always let a glint of their made-ness show through, boiled this basic contract down to its essence in *Batman*.

It was all the more alienating, in the autumn and winter that followed, to hear a Hollywood phrase, which now served at most as an ironic nod at the staged nature of the world, in countless modifications from the mouths of real people: party functionaries and civil rights activists, Stasi staff and writers, clergymen, militaries and Monday demonstrators. Believe me. Trust me. Trust us. But you have to trust us. Why don't you trust us any more?

And every one of those voices tried to give the impression it meant what it said. No one laughed at it – a quote from a film. No one in the East was reminded of Gotham City – I was convinced of that, until I later read that one of the *Batman* producers had, perhaps in typical Hollywood hubris and misinterpretation, realised the true scale of the comic adaptation's success when he saw a young man on TV with the Batman emblem on his hat, moving with the crowd through an opened checkpoint to West Berlin.

That 9 November itself, however, remains a day without me. The longer I circle it, the more it unsettles me not to have kept anything of that date, or at least the previous and subsequent days, in my mind.

I remember a story told by a Dresden friend who had taken part in an expedition to the north of the Soviet Union, as a photographer for the Natural History Collections, and returned to Dresden in early October. For a quarter of a year, his small group had barely seen any people, no radio, no newspapers – and certainly not from the West. As he explored flora and fauna, waited for the best light for his photographs, any idea of current affairs took a back seat; how could that friend have guessed that the familiar conditions at home were eroding?

What the near future would bring had long been printed in the calendar: the fortieth anniversary of the GDR's founding. And there is nothing more boring, in the long run, than a predetermined outcome, for instance the ideal societal system. Until then, you can happily occupy yourself with more interesting things, such as ever-changing nature. Perhaps those responsible for visual agitprop were also beginning to realise, in Dresden in 1988, the crippling effect of predictability, when they had the large neon sign removed from the tower block on Pirnaischer Platz: SOCIALISM SHALL BE VICTORIOUS.

My friend landed at Schönefeld Airport, beyond the outskirts of Berlin, where he might have encountered a sign of changed times. But he took the train straight to Dresden. I don't know whether he simply didn't talk to any other passengers on the way or, immersed in his expedition experiences, he seemed like a man who shouldn't be disturbed. At that time, long-distance trains still stopped at Dresden-Mitte station, not far from his workplace. Had he remained on board until the main station, he would have ended up right inside the historical arena – yet, he had once again only grazed the peripheries of that arena.

But did that even exist: a notion of an arena, even of world events, in the GDR, in Dresden? For those born in the 1950s and 60s, were such events in East Germany not always historical events, Dresden for instance as the arena for the Allied bombing, and did present-day events not always play out elsewhere, no matter what they might be?

In the northern Russian wilderness, my friend had slotted himself into a time structure determined by the rhythm of day and night, the changing of the seasons, and now, crossing time zones, he returned to a world frozen by the proclamation that the further course of history was irrevocably predestined. He returned with uncounted exposed films in his luggage, and he had countless stories to tell. Yet at that point in time, his colleagues at the Natural History Museum, with their precise understanding of evolutionary issues and the geographical spread of species, could not summon up their usual enthusiasm for unknown animals and unfamiliar landscapes.

The main station had been sealed off over the previous nights. A police car had caught fire. Stones had been thrown. The police had clubbed and kettled. Dresdeners had tried to jump onto the trains carrying refugees from the embassy in Prague, routed via Dresden on their way to West Germany, had attempted to occupy the station. My friend knew nothing of this. He had come from the opposite direction and disembarked the train in a present that had taken possession of the city only days before.

I think of those October nights today, when I enter the main station on a Sunday afternoon: the concourse is full of people, everywhere voices and goodbyes, everywhere footsteps, young people thronging the platforms to catch the day's last train west. Even though I didn't learn the details of those trains from Prague until 1996, after I moved to the city, the sight moves me every time: on Sundays, half of Dresden leaves town for West Germany, where the working week begins on Monday morning.

I remember that I spent the last weekend of April 2004 in the West. We were sitting around a table and when I said, 'I'd like to be home right now,' I received quizzical looks. 'They're abolishing passport checks on the borders to Poland and the Czech Republic today; I'd have liked to visit Görlitz or the tri-border region,' I added. Ah, right – nods and murmurs, but I don't think anyone quite understood me.

I wasn't there then. If I look at 9 November 1989 as a historical date, I don't see myself. If I look at myself on that day, the historical events don't come up. My small attic flat in Cologne, the dove-grey carpeting, the TV, a gift from friends: I was sitting on one side of the screen, while on the other side of the convex glass history was happening, right then, at that moment.

Perhaps something began that night, without me being aware of it – perhaps I set out, during the following days of which I have no particular recollection, to examine, by writing, the incompatibility of two images: on the one hand a historic image, entirely contemporary, and there an image depicting me without any trace of history.

*

What never would have been conceivable in the West – not during the Cold War, not after the Cold War: in 1990, lists of the real names, ranks and activities of Stasi employees were hawked out of car boots in the middle of Dresden, six Deutsch-marks per copy.

*

In June 2006, I discover a dusty, guano-stained poster in the main station, emerged from behind a wall panel during renovations: 'David Irving: Expedition into Historical Truth,' it says, 'the world's most-read British historian,' and: 'never proved wrong in 30 years,' along with: 'Tuesday, 5.6.1990 Dresden, Kulturpalast, Am Altmarkt. Wednesday, 6.6.1990 Leipzig, Kongresssaal der AGRA, Mark-Kleeberg. Thursday, 7.6.1990 Gera, Haus der Kultur, Strasse des 7. Oktober. Starting time: 7:30 pm. Entrance: 10 GDR marks for native East Germans, 10 Deutschmarks for West German visitors. You are invited on this unusual journey into historical truth by...' – yes, it really is an invitation to an 'unusual journey,' and were it not a notorious Holocaust denier's speaking tour, I would rub my eyes in disbelief: a Nazi speaker at the Kulturpalast, on 7 October Street. Put sarcastically, regarded soberly: no Western European Nazi would have been stupid enough in 1990 to leave the East hanging, ideologically.

*

'One has to know how to lose – with grandeur.'

VIII

On the late afternoon of 13 October 2005, I get a guided tour of Vilnius in winter sunlight, the medieval town centre, the Black Madonna at Aurora Gate, the Mickiewicz house – the greatest Lithuanian poet writes Polish, or vice versa: the greatest Polish poet comes from Lithuania, provided one doesn't assign him to Constantinople or even Dresden, for simplicity's sake. Then the poet and translator Antanas Gailius leads me along the narrow streets: his paths. Down to the river, towards a church in a pitiful state: 'We didn't have the West here, we have post-socialism.'

At a bus stop, I spot a cat among the waiting passengers, a memento of the dogs I once saw in Kaliningrad as they lay on grey heaps of snow by the side of the road, in the midst of waiting crowds – apparently animals are drawn to bus stops all over the East, in unfamiliar places. At first, I think the cat is approaching passers-by, welcoming every new arrival to its territory and begging for food or contact. Nonetheless, there is a constant distance between human and feline, the waiting people seeming to back off from the cat. Its fur is filthy and full of parasites; it has stopped cleaning itself.

I stop, waiting to see if it will rub its head against my trouser leg. But the cat moves uneasily, as if without purpose. It can barely walk, probably barely hear; in place of eyes are two swollen strips, behind which its pupils must be concealed. It is possible it still senses a path, perceives itself as part of a soundscape, albeit a weak one – I have no other explanation for why it never steps out over the kerb.

The cat is turning to no one, its movements are merely automatic; all remaining signs of its felinity – its arched back and the footsteps that bring it close to me – have nothing to do with me. Anyone can tell it will not survive the coming winter. The last light will bid farewell to the cat; the soundscape will release it into nowhere. What I ask myself over and over during the next few days: In the head of a cat, like that of a human, do inner voices grow louder as the sounds of the outside world quieten down?

I do not see myself reflected in this animal, do not identify with it; nor is it an allegory, be it for the city, the century, life and literature. I would have wanted to describe the cat, its squat figure, its no longer even tentative gait, the run-down fur, the germ-ridden ears, the blind eyes in its destroyed face. Just as I see it before me in great clarity to this day: the Vilnius cat, utterly re-immersed in itself; a cat concealed inside a cat.

*

It is raining. 30 March 2006. That afternoon in the Old Masters restaurant, behind the Zwinger with a view of the opera, I think I recognise Imre Kertész at the next table. The stature is not quite right, nor the hairline, but the eyes are, and the way he's sitting, I convince myself. Between coffee cup and finished ice-cream sundae is a city map of Dresden, a travel guide in French, but the couple's conversation – neither he nor she native speakers – is in English. Of course, it is not 'the' Imre Kertész, but as I try to capture the tone while half-listening, first it's a French-Canadian, then a Monégasque, a Basque and finally a Macedonian Imre Kertész. I almost think he would, were I to seek eye contact, make perfectly clear to me: think a little longer, you've nearly found out which Imre Kertész I am.

'The "I" is a fiction and we can be at best its co-authors,' Kertész writes in the early 1990s, placing this sentence, in quotation marks and initialled 'I. K.', at the beginning of his notes, as though it had not originated in the book but had sought its way in from somewhere outside, to be chronicled between front matter and notes. In the text, then, we read it alongside Arthur Rimbaud's 'I is someone else,' and that dictum, too, has found its place among mottos. In altered form, it also provides the book's title: *Someone Else*, Tim Wilkinson's English version retaining the Hungarian subtitle jettisoned by the German edition: *A Chronicle of the Change*.

'JE est un autre,' beginning uppercase in the original: a core 20th-century sentence originating in the 19th century, and usually little more than a radical-sounding but cosy slogan, but as soon as we try to discard the existential dimension along with that personal pronoun, the threatening undertone of 'I was not quite myself' creeps in.

Swiss German, in places where it's strongly influenced by French, has this everyday phrase: *s Schöberli het gseit* – little-I, tiny me said. Perhaps, from the Viennese couch, High German's *ich* and its object the *es* – ego and id – have now been so loaded with meaning for a century that we ('we' – co-authors at best) might hear Rimbaud's words as a simple reversal of the swift, barely noticed shift from object into subject: *moi, je*. Two syllables that start countless French sentences every day.

Pay less attention to the 'I', the advice goes –however, it once again claims attention, as in the equally over-quoted words of

Walter Benjamin: 'If I write better German than most writers of my generation, it is thanks largely to 20 years' observation of one little rule: never use the word "I" except in letters.' The second word of this now aphoristic passage from the *Berlin Chronicles*: 'I'.

'Except in letters': Where is Rimbaud's best-known sentence to be found? Not in his prose, not in a poem – let us recall his obscure last lines of verse, which are basically: 'I am Swiss cheese.' Arthur Rimbaud formulates 'I is someone else' on 15 May 1871 in a letter from the town of his birth, Charleville. And what if Benjamin, having written his last full stop, had remembered that? Over the course of the following sentences, he will – in grammar and thought – lose his way a little, finally breaking off abruptly his thoughts for a 'foreword', one that – he writes – has long since ballooned to more than a foreword, just as he will later break off work on his *Berlin Chronicles* – or, more precisely, rework it into his *Berlin Childhood around 1900*. As if he had stared, as he went on writing, transfixed at that 'I' at the beginning, half disappointed at having formulated a so-so style-guide sentence ('a letter never begins with an "I"'), half surprised as he watches the 'I' involuntarily shifting once it has found its way from his hand onto the paper: when you write, every 'I' automatically becomes an object, and through the eyes of the writer any object can also be observed as an 'I'.

To be shown such a shift, one can read Adalbert Stifter's *Granite*: 'One of the most recent members of our house to sit upon that stone was I, in my boyhood.' Or the entertainer Harald Juhnke's 'autobiography' with the rather feline title *My Seven Lives*, its first sentences – spotlights on a figure in a desolate state, in the third person – resulting in the 'confession': this person is 'I'. Whereby here, the 'I' is literally an observed 'I', as Juhnke's exasperated ghost writer Harald Wieser once explained: he had had to find a way to make the mute character by the name of Harald Juhnke speak on paper. Similar to Charles Mingus, who at the beginning of *Beneath the Underdog*, in the first person, observes 'my boy', the young Charles Mingus himself – or is it the ghost writer speaking here, too, from the very beginning?

'If I write better German than most writers of my generation' – nothing seems to connect this 1932 formulation with the first sentence of the actual 'foreword' that Walter Benjamin will later place at the front of his *Berlin Childhood around 1900*: 'In 1932, when I was abroad, it began to be clear to me that I would soon have to bid a long, perhaps lasting farewell to the city of my birth.'

In the meantime, writers of his generation have decreed it is no longer 'worse' or 'better German' – in other words style – that determines quality, but a substance, albeit an entirely imaginary one: 'blood'. According to that logic, 'I' is always the same – 'blood', unlike style, cannot be improved. Everything has been decided in advance, countless generations ago, and thus the examination of language, the 'struggle' for style, even any competition between writers for 'better German' all lose their meaning. One can tell that by the racial fanatics' careless use of language, tell by the fact that not a sentence in their books written between 1933 and 1945 is palatable, and one can experience it on the basis of the severe discrepancy between the boast of Germanness and linguistic ability, every day on the tram. 'I is a German', and language courses are for other people.

Benjamin takes his now 'incomparable' German abroad, into the company of other languages, where he examines the 'lasting farewell' from the city of his birth, the place where he learned his German. Walter Benjamin's better German cannot

167

be ascribed to the rule 'never to use the word "I",' as he will have noted himself. How else could his *Berlin Childhood*, that 'I'-book, have become Benjamin's most linguistically dense, darkest, most sparkling work, one of the most important German-language books of the past century. Benjamin leaves the space where his language is spoken and the 'ich' comes to the fore, oscillating between subject and object, between German personal pronoun and imagined identity. And his homeland – does it emigrate with him, or does it stay behind?

On 7 March 1875, a small ad appears in the *Schwäbische Kronik*, Stuttgart – its sensational rediscovery due to Ute Harbusch – it reads: 'A Parisian, 20 y. old, would be inclined to study the German language versus French with persons eager to learn.'

Whether the placer of the ad formulated the text alone or had help from his landlord – Herr Wagner, in whose home he inhabits, by his own statement, 'a friendly room' – we do not know. I note the brief 'versus' in the sense of 'in exchange for'; someone wants to 'take' German lessons and at the same time 'give' French: 'Little-I said.'

Language for language – who, then, is 'I'? In this case, a young Frenchman who has lit up the language of poetry to this day, who is just abandoning poetry at that time: 'Letters to A. Rimbaud, Hasenbergstr. 7, Stuttgart.' I is a language-learner improving his German abroad.

'The green wallpaper of the hotel room in the Dresden dusk. Outside heavy rainfall.' It is May. Imre Kertész is accommodated in the Interhotel Neva, between Prager and Leningrader Strasse, a room with a view of the main station. The terminal building, he says, gave him a sense of déja-vu from the very beginning, but he cannot quite place it. In his suitcase, an unfinished novel; Kertész begins to read the existing pages of *Fiasco* – a manuscript about the rejection of a manuscript, *Fatelessness*.

As if incidentally, he notes that the state of the *Fiasco* pages fits in well with the 'visible ruins here'. A little later, however, emerging from his reading, he is guided by these fragments to the intact concourse beyond the station forecourt, and the written word sheds light, via detours, on memory: from here, Kertész took the train 'home' to Budapest when he came out of Buchenwald in 1945.

Late May 1980, rain, green wallpaper: Imre Kertész has brought his language along to Dresden. Perhaps that is one reason why he writes better German than many writers of his generation, even though he uses Hungarian.

*

With the vague, essentially insane idea that Tadeusz Borowski might say something about Dresden, I open up *This Way for the Gas, Ladies and Gentlemen* at a random page in the middle and come directly upon the sentence: 'By then, they'll have improved the gas ovens, they'll be more economical to use and better camouflaged. They'll be like the ones in Dresden, of which people already tell stories today.'

*

What kind of people, when they hear of the horrors of the 20th century, of systematic contempt for humankind, psychological annihilation and torture, demand of the person telling them that he ought to have experienced it all at first hand? They can't all be emotional sadists, surely.

When I tell someone about things beyond my and their experience, it is not uncommon for my interlocutor to refer to another writer, nodding, and thus strangely affirming what I've said: 'He described it much more drastically. And also experienced it himself.' How their little eyes light up. I take an involuntary step back.

*

In the Semmelweis Museum in Budapest, I saw a taxidermised child hidden in the library.

*

The Natural History Museum in Bucharest keeps the urns containing the ashes of the museum's founder Grigore Antipa, who died in 1944, and his wife Alina, in a small, glazed niche in the wall at adult eye level. They are easily overlooked as one leaves the exhibition rooms on the ground floor and turns to the large staircase in the entrance hall to ascend to the first floor.

*

Once in a lifetime, to Stendal. A French writer crosses Europe in Napoleon's retinue and adopts – for reasons of camouflage? as a sign of his worldliness? – the slightly altered name of a place in the Altmark as his pseudonym.

I've never visited Stendal, but I come across the writer's name everywhere in the late 20th and early 21st century: in Vilnius, I stand outside a house in which Stendhal stayed on his way to Moscow in 1812. In his *Memoirs of an Egotist*, he mentions he had the idea for a novel he never wrote down in Dresden in 1813, and I presume I could also have found a plaque near Kaliningrad, where Stendhal's sleigh once cracked the ice as he was crossing the frozen Vistula Lagoon.

Whenever I leave the narrow valley of Lower Valais behind me, coming from Lake Geneva, and reach Martigny, I pass the turn-off for Saint Bernhard's Pass – and think of Stendhal: so vividly does he picture himself crossing the Alps to the south from here, that he begins to doubt whether he's actually describing his own memories, and not a pictorial presentation of this mountainous area; an engraving he first saw several years after his experience.

In Parma, we spend a night at the Hotel Stendhal; in Rome, we are drawn on Saturday afternoons to the Piazzale delle Province, where we watch the whole neighbourhood parade past, the sound of weekend traffic in the background. We sit outside an establishment that has both the writer and the place in its name: the printing on the awnings reads 'Bar Stendal', while on the paper napkins it is called 'Stendhal Bar'. The nearby bus station offers direct connections to Minsk.

*

Minsk, late September 2009. In no other city have I ever felt as foreign. Not in Kiev, not in Nanjing, not in Hiroshima. Or is it down to me? – have I become exhausted by the East? Barely have I closed the hotel-room door behind me on arrival, before the obligatory call comes: 'Do you feel lonely?'

In the post-socialist age – which has not yet even dawned in Belarus – the secret service doesn't speak through a mouth on first approach; the secret service speaks through a vagina. There's no other option but to unplug the telephone.

My aggressive unease may be to do with the fact that I have crossed an outer border of the European Union by land for the first time in – how many? – years, arriving by train from Lithuania. Miles of floodlights in a corridor narrowing towards the border, made insurmountable by razor wire, in the midst of the September landscape. Radio was playing on the train, a Belarusian rap number with a loop of *Für Elise*; I stood smoking by the door of the last carriage, leaning my head against the closed door, and saw kilometres of border facilities from the Cold War, which was supposed to be long over. And I heard in my head the German line from T. S. Eliot's *The Waste Land*: 'Bin gar keine Russin, stamm' aus Litauen, echt deutsch.'

Am I feeling shut in or out? And who, in either case, would *I* be?

In Vilnius – my only plan for my second stay in the city – I looked for the place where I'd seen the 'Vilnius cat' four years earlier. At noon I recognised, not far from the three churches making up the 'Gothic ensemble', a freshly mown lawn in the autumn sunlight and in front of it the footpath, the bus stop, the road – that is, I recognised nothing except the location of this place, because the cobbles had been replaced by asphalt, every paving stone by another paving stone, and one might almost think every blade of grass by another blade of grass. A new bus stop. No one waiting. And – what had I expected? – of course no withdrawn, invalid cat, which presumably no one in the world remembers but me.

So, do I feel shut in or out here in Minsk? On my key card, the Hotel Yubileiny makes a very different impression to the Hotel Express in Kiev. Were anyone to devote themselves to such an idiotic undertaking as a search for 'national character', they ought at least to restrict their study material to hotel key cards: there the concrete tower rising to a pale-blue spring sky in Kiev, here the almost identical hotel building in Minsk – photographed, however, in strange greenish-red colouring. Is it due to bad printing, or do they want to make a vague impression here? Hardly anything can be seen clearly – the photo seems blurred, a row of four windows shining dully on the top floor, but I couldn't even say precisely how many storeys the Yubileiny has.

The view from my sixth-floor window – not much more than vastness. Three six-lane roads, on the left a yellowish housing estate forms the horizon, on the right a wooded area that looks suspiciously as though the president once wished for a wood as he drove past this spot.

A closed world. Here a Potemkin forest, there a Potemkin town centre. It is not just because this city was destroyed to a greater extent than almost any other in Europe during the war. One senses: its shape obeys the whims of a single person.

When I leave my room, my eyes alight on a gigantic propaganda poster, outside the windows by the lift. It extends across several storeys of the adjacent building, two soldiers raising – in an enlarged photo or a photorealistic painting – the Belarusian flag. Another indication that the president passes this hotel on his way into town. I'm about to press the button to summon the lift when my attention is caught by an art print – typical hotel corridor decoration, I think at first, like one sees everywhere. Then, however, it is suddenly as though the world were expanding, as though something had been waiting for me here. No, I'm not looking at a reproduction of *Jockel*, Grohmann's last dog; it's an offset print of a Kandinsky piece, and its title is, in large letters: *Ommagio a Grohmann*.

This *I* is the first person to bring something along: images, words, names.

And this *I* is the short-tempered man who doesn't recognise himself the next morning, as he abandons all decency on the station forecourt in Minsk, in the coming and going of travellers, taxi drivers and loiterers, as part of a group meeting here for a walking tour of the city; this man who yells out of nowhere at a German journalist holding his Dictaphone to the interpreter's mouth, who then speaks quieter and quieter, lowers her head to the microphone so the other listeners soon can no longer identify a word of her already hard-to-understand English – in the traffic noise, the buzz of Belarusian voices on the station forecourt – let alone assemble the words into meaningful sentences. I fly off the handle; I snap at a stranger in strange surroundings, loudly enough to be audible not only to those standing around me but also to the passers-by, who turn around quizzically – no: who turn away and accelerate their pace. Who is this man looking another in the eye and yelling: 'Turn off your fucking Dictaphone or I'll throw it in the bloody road,' whereupon the tour guide and the interpreter and all those gathered around them fall silent, in the middle of one of the most crowded places in Minsk, a city mute despite its traffic noise and buzz of voices?

'This short-tempered man who doesn't recognise himself' – that's not true. If I don't recognise myself, then only in retrospect, whereas in the situation outside the station, my aggression is fed partly by the momentary conviction of being the only person to do the right thing, the *only* right thing. What is worst about my outbreak – never before, never since have I behaved so violently – is thus, perhaps, that I am not even a stranger to myself while I do it.

This is me, then. I'm trembling all over. I've left no room for doubt that I mean it; I really would smash the Dictaphone against the road between the cars. After a while, someone asks quietly: 'Are you alright now?'

My justification to myself and the others seems absolutely coherent to me. Of course, I was irritated because I wanted to follow what the tour guide was saying, I claim – but beyond that fervour, I cobble up a 'bigger picture' as I speak, which makes my behaviour appear inevitable. How could anyone, I ask, in a country where every action is monitored, where every word is listened in on and possibly recorded, hold a microphone under a local person's nose, and in broad daylight? What if the recordings 'fell into someone's hands' who used them not only against the journalist, but first and foremost against his interviewee? We've already been told that the secret service regularly 'visits' the private homes even of foreigners holding diplomatic protection – how foolish must someone be to think he could hide his Dictaphone in the hotel room, for instance, under the mattress – 'Do you feel lonely?'

I act like someone who resorts to violence only to protect third parties. To protect whom, though? Representatives of the Belarusian opposition? The residents of Minsk? The Belarusian people? Absurd. I don't even know whether I've come across any representatives of the opposition. Whether I've heard words that might cost someone dearly. Nonetheless, I'm convinced I'm in the right.

And yet, seen without the emotion of the moment, the opposite is the case: I was perfectly willing to destroy the tools of a journalist using a rare opportunity to capture voices in Minsk outside the official communiqués. In Belarus, I turned into my own totalitarian state.

As though someone from our group – and not, for instance, a Belarusian secret policeman – had threatened to take my notebook full of observations of Minsk and burn it then and there.

When I finally apologise to the journalist on our return to Tegel Airport and add that I behaved like a swine and there can be no apology for that, I am not relieved. I'm still not.

*

In unfamiliar lands, our own language proves to be the untameable lion itself? Before leaving Minsk, I visit not the Zoological Garden on Sunday afternoon, like the Dostoevskys might have done, but the Historical Museum, where I've been told there is at least a small zoological section on the lower floor. Who

175

knows? – perhaps even a taxidermised lion can be encouraged to roar if one only looks long and deep enough into its big glass eyes.

But I don't see lions, giraffes or even a mere flock of gentle gazelles – the animal world is restricted entirely to the local fauna, as everything in Belarus seems to be related solely to Belarus and, beyond that, to Big Brother Russia. The question is which stands for which when the stuffed fox carries off a stuffed black grouse, or when the large bird of prey squeezed into a case between its relatives holds a dead mole in its talons.

My first stop is an exhibition dedicated to the history of humankind: bones and shards and arrowheads, primordial man behind glass, and a reconstructed library in the last room. I pay little attention to the exhibits – they don't speak to me, because the Belarusian and Russian commentary on the accompanying signs are impenetrable for me. Aside from that, a group of visitors distracts me: two dozen soldiers in dress uniform, clustered around the cabinets of historical weapons at the rear end of the section. The museum guide has trouble luring them away to the shelf where, as I suspected, outstanding examples of scholarly works important for Belarus or originating from Belarus are displayed. Between the uniforms, I catch a glimpse at the Latin front matter of an opened folio and turn to the exit – that is: to a low, brown-painted door, which I'm not sure isn't an entrance to forbidden rooms. I turn the knob cautiously, but it won't open. So I turn around and find the entrance back into the corridor, which branches off from a different room.

I wander rather aimlessly, though the museum is too small to get lost, and a little later a friendly museum attendant takes me aside – she has been watching me for a while, no doubt, and now talks at me, yes, talks all the more at me the clearer I try to make it that I don't understand a word she's saying.

How could I explain that I'm looking neither for a poppy, backlit presentation of Belarusian steppe grasses nor for the main work of a Belarusian astronomer, but for the zoological section? She, however, will not be dissuaded from helping me, and points at a small, brown-painted door, which I immediately recognise: behind it is the room I saw at the beginning. I shake my head, I shrug my shoulders, then I simply tell her I've been there already, speaking German with a friendly expression: 'Da war ich.'

'Ah,' she says, as if I'd not only expressed myself clearly at last, but spoken human language for the first time in our exchange. 'Ah,' and nods, and points at the door, and repeats: 'Da war ich,' or: 'Davarich,' or: 'Davarishch,' whereupon she dismisses me, fully satisfied.

I don't know what she understood, but it does occur to me that I'm welcomed particularly courteously by the attendant in the animal section a little later. Indeed, as I eye the stuffed wood grouse and great tits in their dioramas, it seems as though a museum worker, having addressed a few polite words to me, the only visitor in the section, vanishes with particular respect behind a concealed door between two glass cases, to slip swiftly and soundlessly into a more presentable pair of shoes. As though she didn't wish to disturb this wildly drivelling guest.

And yes, language has suddenly gone wild again, as I piece together after the fact, not wild and dangerous this time, but wild and beautiful, between the stuffed and silent beasts: presumably, in my excitement, in the unfamiliar linguistic surroundings, in the attempt to explain to an attendant that I already knew the room behind the brown door, I had without realising adopted the Rhineland inflection that surrounded me for twenty-three years, and articulated instead of a clear, High German 'Da war ich' a slurred, over-emphasised 'Da'varisch'. And revealed myself

177

in the ears of the museum ladies as a 'davaritsch', 'tovarishch', an upstanding party comrade.

*

For the journey home from the airport, I take my time to choose a pleasant-looking taxi driver. I wait, first of all, for the first car in line to have picked up a passenger; I smoke another cigarette and then the second and third taxis are gone, and with them the mental images of meat sandwiches on the passenger seat, tree-shaped air fresheners, and shirts worn since early that morning.

The first driver in a long time not to ask me whether I've been to Dresden before. For the first 10 years, barely any of them assumed that I, not a speaker of the Saxon dialect, was a visitor from elsewhere. Now, though, even subtle hints like my question about the last three days' weather – obviously during my absence, surely? – or a comment on a never-ending building site down in the valley go ignored. And with every year that passes, it grows harder for me to explain, yes, I've lived in this city for 12, 13, 14 or for 15 years. Giving this information means asking myself, every time, who I am.

My chauffeur for this drive, however, instantly gets the message, since I don't give him a hotel name but a street and an address as destination, that I am coming home from far away – which on this occasion happens to be the place of my birth. Politely, he asks whether I travel a lot, and we exchange a few words.

When he hears I'm a writer he has an urgent question, which sounds like a mere comment, so reticently does he ask it, his gaze sliding through the rear-view mirror: 'Book by Karl May with three letters.'

I know all taxi drivers pass the waiting time with crossword puzzles, and I know the correct answer, and yet I have to think

for a moment how to give it to him without seeming strange –
like a madman or like someone who can't help referring every
question to himself: '*Ich*,' I say, 'that must be *Ich*.'

Many thanks to the Deutsche Akademie Villa Massimo Rom. Without the year of cheerful withdrawal spent in the best, always stimulating company in Rome in 2010, this book would not exist, even though it was neither written nor conceived there.

Putin's Postbox came about between October 2003 and October 2011, and includes extracts from a number of published works:

'Putins Briefkasten'. In: *Frankfurter Allgemeine Sonntagszeitung*, 5 October 2003, p. 34.

'Narva, Anoraks'. Talk in the Café Europa at the sixth Kosmopolis International Literature Festival in Barcelona, 22 October 2006.

'Laßt mich nach Zaspa gehen'. In: *Sarmatische Landschaften. Nachrichten aus Litauen, Belarus, der Ukraine, Polen und Deutschland.* Edited by Martin Pollack. Frankfurt / M.: S. Fischer 2005, pp. 28–37.

'Filme der Frühzeit'. Talk at the Literary Colloquium Berlin, 14 December 2005. In: *Sprache im technischen Zeitalter* No. 179, September 2006, pp. 242–254.

'Pieter Claesz, Jelenia Góra'. In: *Bilder. Geschichten. Schriftsteller sehen Malerei.* Edited by Thomas Böhm and Andreas Blühm. Munich: Luchterhand 2006, pp. 55–63.

'Lessings Ofenschirm'. In: *Mit Lessing ins Gespräch.* Edited by Heinz Ludwig Arnold. Göttingen: Wallstein 2004, pp. 79–83.

'Benzin'. In: *DC: Heike Beyer: Bergfink.* Museum Ludwig, Cologne. Cologne: Verlag der Buchhandlung Walther König 2004, pp. 9–13.

'Scheinfrühling'. In: *Vom Ohrenbeben zu Edenkoben.* Edited by Gregor Laschen. Heidelberg: Wunderhorn 2007, pp. 38f.

'Brixton'. In: *Das erste Buch. Schriftsteller über ihr literarisches Debüt.* Edited by Renatus Deckert. Frankfurt / M.: Suhrkamp 2007, pp. 220–225.

'Gedichte, Blicke, Bälge. Die Ornithologie und das Handwerk des Lyrikers'. In: *Neue Zürcher Zeitung,* 20/21 March 2004, pp. 61f.

'An der Sprachgrenze'. Acceptance speech for the Spycher Prize, awarded in Leuk, Valais, on 26 September 2004. In: *Neue Zürcher Zeitung,* 5/6 February 2005, p. 45.

'Psyche läßt sich auf den Worten nieder'. In: *Verleihung des Siegfried-Unseld-Preises an Inger Christensen am 28. September 2006.* Private printing. Frankfurt/M.: Suhrkamp, Insel 2007, pp. 27–32.

'Mein Bienenjahr lesen'. In: *Erst lesen. Dann schreiben. 22 Autoren und ihre Lehrmeister*. Edited by Olaf Kutzmutz and Stephan Porombka. Munich: Luchterhand 2007, pp. 214–232.

'Wilhelm Müller: Tafelgeheimnisse'. In: *Künstler in Dresden im 20. Jahrhundert*. Literarische Porträts. Edited by Wulf Kirsten and Hans-Peter Lühr. Husum: Verlag der Kunst Dresden 2005, pp. 154–158.

'Ein Tag ohne mich'. In: *Die Nacht, in der die Mauer fiel. Schriftsteller erzählen vom 9. November 1989*. Edited by Renatus Deckert. Frankfurt/M.: Suhrkamp 2009, pp. 148–158.

'Die Katze von Vilnius'. In: *Bella triste* No. 15, Summer 2006, pp. 64–69.

Translator's Note

It is raining. 30 November 2020. Marcel Beyer leads me around
the outside of an unremarkable block of flats in Dresden. Raindrops glint on the varnish of parked cars beneath the streetlamps
as the dusk overtakes our leisurely footsteps. We are in no rush;
Putin and his postbox have long gone. We see no one, hear no
Russian, English or German voices; on this gloomy Monday during Germany's 'lockdown light', people are occupied inside their
own four walls, with no need for anecdotal material over their
evening meals. The block is Stammheim-grey, guano-stained,
with yellow curtains at the ground-floor windows. It seems perfectly feasible that Vladimir Putin should have lived here during
his time with the KGB, yet impalpably far away in time.

We visit, too, Putin's former workplace on Angelikastrasse,
now a 'Rudolf-Steiner-Haus' and not keen to advertise its previous incarnation as KGB headquarters. Cropped lawns around
a neat villa, but security is still high; the library is open for a
single hour a week, as we read between the raindrops on the

glazed noticeboard outside. A few hundred yards around the corner, once we've crossed a dual carriageway, followed by two pairs of tram lines, followed by another dual carriageway – cars' tyres spraying water and sound as they pass, rendering conversation impossible beyond shouted suggestions of when to venture across – we reach the much larger, far more imposing former Stasi premises. My red umbrella drips outside the 'Fox's Den'. We don't go inside.

'I'm sure the poet's gaze is much clearer in *Putin's Postbox* than the novelist's, whereby I've also noticed or found out, over the course of the past 15 years, that essays offer a marvellous opportunity to tell stories without plot. For example, there's a word that seems strange to you, and you find that word in another place in the world and you don't have to create a hero and his social surroundings, a narrative arc; you can burrow from one word to another as if under the earth, and pop up again somewhere else,' Beyer says in an interview for Deutschlandfunk.

There is much of this burrowing and leaping from one word to the next in these essays, as you'll have noticed. Usually, that presents no major challenges to a translator, who by default is happy to go where words lead her. In places, though, it demands a freer translation, such as where our disgruntled narrator subtly emphasises the link between VWs and fascism: 'A word like "silencer", a word like "clutch", a word like "boot"' – those weren't direct translations. In place of fenders, windscreen washer systems and passenger compartments, the German words for which have a distinct whiff of the concentration camp, I looked for threatening-sounding car parts.

Most difficult and yet most exciting, however, was the essay on beekeeping books. Where the writer's joy lies precisely in *not* understanding the terminology, I felt I needed to know more; the translator must weigh up whether sound or meaning should take precedence. This is always true, of course, but when translating a poet's gaze, such decisions become more complex. I had to be sure I could find the corresponding terms before either adopting or discarding them. The language of beekeeping is as arcane as it is delightful, and the internet is awash with glossaries. How, though, could I trust any particular one? Even if I *thought* I had the right word, was I sure I was using it correctly?

My friend and fellow translator Bill Martin alerted me to the existence of a *Dictionary of Beekeeping Terms* published by the Apimondia International Bee Research Association; the edition I bought used is Volume 7: English-German-Dutch-Danish-Norwegian-Swedish, published in 1978 in Bucharest 'with allied scientific terms' and edited by Eva Crane. Its pages are thin and shiny and smell faintly of cheese, between linen-bound covers the colour of oxidised English mustard. There are three columns on each page, taking us, for instance, from *to transfer (bees)* to *umlogieren* to *overbrengen* and then across the stitching to *at omhuse* to *å overføre* to *att överflytta*. The languages echo brightly – Marcel, I am sure, would covet it too. With Eva Crane's help, I managed to translate Marcel's paean to Lieselotte Gettert, initially without the unwanted baggage of understanding every word. Where I felt sound was fundamental, I could flick through and find a more fitting choice. Further research reassured me I had made no major blunders in terms of meaning.

The other major challenge of the translation was identifying the many quotes in the book, then locating English versions of them. I am thankful for the existence of the Internet Archive, without which I suspect this translation could not have been done. Working in physical libraries, finding German and English editions of the 19 different publications listed overleaf and those credited in the text itself might have taken years. Where possible, I chose older translations rather than the sometimes more accurate re-translations now available, which would usually be my preference; I felt that was in keeping with the essays' playful spirit.

There were some sources for which no English translation has ever been published; in these cases, I translated the German quotes directly. In one particularly frustrating case, several paragraphs had been omitted from an English translation published in the 1970s, including the very section I was seeking. In another, both the Polish and the German terms for a particular part of a carriage – *wałek* and *Walze* – proved utterly opaque to me, encompassing a huge range of potential meanings. Here, I was helped by my colleagues Esther Kinsky and Zofia Sucharska, both of whom spent several hours in total puzzling with me and consulting old photographs, over what eventually became a 'padded cylinder'.

I am also grateful, as always, to my editor Florian Duijsens for all his wise interventions, and to Angela Hirons for adding clarity and beauty. Many thanks also to the Berliner Senat for the timely research grant.

As one of the points where languages rub up against each other, the translator's work can be more challenging than it might appear. This particular translation was part intuitive, part investigative. It tested me and stretched me, and I hope it has made me a better translator.

In January 2021, Alexei Navalny's team release a two-hour video investigation into 'Putin's Palace', allegedly a new Versailles, a separate state inside Russia, built for the president. While Navalny himself has returned to Russia from Germany, having recovered in hospital from poisoning, and is now in prison, we see him sitting on a bench outside a pastel-yellow housing block. A little patch of pink flashes above his left shoulder: an old woman observing him from an upper window. This, he tells us in subtitled Russian, is where Vladimir Putin once lived during his time in Dresden. How strange; can they have painted the block in the month or two since I was there? It is certainly the same place. Looking at it now, almost a year later, I am no longer sure what colour the building was when we visited it. Did I imagine that dreary grey, the rain marking the concrete walls? Was it raining at all? Am I, perhaps, a narrator as unreliable as Marcel Beyer's, a borrower of styles, an imitator of images?

I am a translator, I say. Simply a translator.

Katy Derbyshire, November 2021

Where sources were not originally in English, I have used the following translations:

Louis Aragon, Jean Cocteau: *Conversations on the Dresden Gallery*, tr. Francis Scarfe. New York: Holmes and Meier, 1982

Juan Benet: *La construcción de la torre de Babel*. Madrid: Ediciones Siruela, 1990. Own translation from German (*Der Turmbau zu Babel*, tr. Gerhard Poppenberg. Frankfurt: Suhrkamp Verlag, 1994)

Walter Benjamin: *Childhood*, tr. Howard Eiland. Cambridge, MA: Harvard University Press, 2006

Walter Benjamin: *Chronicles*, tr. Edmund Jephcott. New York: Schocken Books, 1978

Tadeusz Borowski, *Pożegnanie z Marią*. Warsaw: Spółdzielnia Wydawnicza "Wiedza", 1948. Own translation from German (*Die steinerne Welt*, tr. Vera Czerny. Munich: Piper Verlag, 1963). Section omitted from English translation (*This Way for the Gas, Ladies and Gentlemen*, tr. Barbara Vedder. London: Penguin, 1976)

Elias Canetti: *The Conscience of Words*, tr. Joachim Neugröschel. New York: Farrar Straus Giroux, 1984

Paul Celan: *Briefwechsel*, own translation. Frankfurt/ M.: Suhrkamp Verlag, 2001

Marguerite Duras *The War: A Memoir*, tr. Barbara Bray. London: William Collins, 1986

Gustave Flaubert: *Madame Bovary*, tr. Geoffrey Wall. London: Penguin, 1992

Karl von Frisch: *The Dancing Bees*, tr. Dora Ilse. London: Methuen, 1954

Johann Wolfgang von Goethe: 'Erl-King', in *Poems of Goethe: Translated in the Original Metres*, tr. Edgar Alfred Bowring. New York: J.W. Lovell Company, 1899

Zygmunt Haupt: *Pierścień z papieru*. Wołowiec: Wydawnictwo Czarne, 1997. Own translation from German (*Ein Ring aus Papier*, tr. Esther Kinsky. Frankfurt/ M.: Suhrkamp Verlag, 2003)

Gotthold Ephraim Lessing: 'The Vision', in *Fables*, translator uncredited. London: John Taylor, 1829

Mandelstam: 'Voz'mi na radost'', in: *Stolen Air: Selected Poems of Osip Mandelstam*, tr. Christian Wiman. New York: Ecco, 2012

Fernando Pessoa: *The Book of Disquiet*, tr. Margaret Jull Costa. London: Serpent's Tail, 2017

Plato: *The Dialogues of Plato*, tr. Benjamin Jowett. Oxford: Oxford University Press 1892

Marcel Proust: *Remembrance of Things Past*, tr. C. K. Scott Moncrieff. New York: Random House, 1927

Marcel Proust on Maeterlinck, tr. Chris Taylor: http://www.yorktaylors.free-online.co.uk/

Adalbert Stifter: *Motley Stones*, tr. Isabel Cole. New York: New
York Review Books, 2021